# The Secret Art of Poisoning

The True Crimes of Martha Needle, the Richmond Poisoner

The Secret Art of Poisoning

EPUB: 9780648372806
POD: 9780648372813

Cover design by Red Tally Studios
Photos: Australian Manuscripts Collection, State Library of Victoria; National Centre
of Biography, Australian National University. PROV. VPRS 516/P0002 Central Register
of Female Prisoners 1857 - 1948. (VPRS 516/P0002, Unit 11, Prisoner No.s 5926 -
6415, Needle Martha: No. 6327, page 409, Year 1894); Hansen Yuncken; Samantha
Battams

Publishing services provided by Critical Mass
www.critmassconsulting.com

# 1

# Introduction

In 2009 I was perusing copies of *The Adelaide Chronicle* of 1920 which told of the historic first ever UK to Australia flight undertaken by the Smith Brothers of South Australia whose journey finally ended in aviator Captain Harry Butler's airport north of Adelaide. As I carefully leafed through the fragile and pungent pages of the old newspaper, I was also taken by a series of large articles all headed under *'The Rhynie Tragedy'*, a story which at the time appeared bigger than the heroic Smith Brothers' celebrated landing in their home state. These articles told the tale of the murder of three children and their mother in Rhynie, a small town near Auburn, in what is now the Clare Valley wine region.

Staring out under the headlines of *The Adelaide Chronicle*[1] article were three very similar and chubby young children: Raymond, Ina and Walter Lee. Raymond Lee most resembled his father, Alexander Newland Lee, whose image appeared on the adjacent page. Alexander was a handsome looking man who looked like a respectable citizen in his sharp Railways Department uniform, complete with shining shoes and cap. He

---

1    The Adelaide Chronicle, 1 May, 1920.

was also the alleged murderer – via strychnine poisoning – of three of his children and his wife. He spared an older girl, eight year old Amelia, whom he had recently taken on a trip to Adelaide from Marrabel, and 18 month-old Alice, and his newborn twins Ronald and Dorothy were perhaps saved by chance as they were sick in the Mareeba Hospital.

I carefully leafed through the pages of the old newspaper to read further articles on the case. Alexander grew up at 'World's End', Kooringa, Burra, north of Adelaide. He was a destitute shearer who had injured his hand in a shearing accident, leaving his large family with little means of survival. Shortly before the murders, whilst in Adelaide for treatment for his hand, Alexander suggested in letters to his wife that he had nothing to live for. But earlier in February, whilst in the Willows Hospital[2] in the Barossa Valley for five weeks, Alexander had fallen for the daughter of the man who ran the hospital, a young nurse of Prussian (German) descent who had cared for him, Vera 'Dolly' Scholz.

Alexander Lee's crimes appeared to be motivated by the desperate situation of his injured hand affecting his livelihood and that of his large family, his jealousy of his wife's relationship to his brother whom the whole family was economically dependent upon (and who was planning to move away), his infatuation with his nurse 'Dolly', and was spurred by his sociopathic lack of empathy for his wife and children.

The criminal court trial held in Adelaide in June was eagerly awaited, so much so that the public was lined up outside the court before each session, waiting to get in. The court was subsequently packed with regular citizens scandalised by every detail of *The Rhynie Tragedy*. The case

---

2    Ran by Dr Scholz and founded with money from George Fife Angas, it is
     now the beautiful Willows Vineyard.

largely rested on the evidence of poor young Amelia, and the pressure on her was palpable. Also featuring in the news was one of Alexander's brothers who was an upright citizen[3] who commented to the press that if the law didn't deal with his brother, then he would. During the trial, innocent 'Dolly' Scholz was accused of being a prostitute and her brother a pimp by the defendant's legal team. Meanwhile, Alexander pleaded his innocence to the end.

Lee was found guilty by a Jury and the date set for the hanging was 15th July 1920, the birthday of the Reverend who was counselling Lee in prison. This was also the day when the HRH Prince of Wales would be in Adelaide. The Premier expressed his regret that the hanging was to occur on this day. An impassioned public debate on the case ensued. Many letters were sent to the daily newspapers, for and against capital punishment, with it being declared a 'relic of the dark ages,' 'barbarism' and the 'most ghoulish, ghastly and inhuman law that was ever placed in our statute books.' Some letters were more personal and asked the state government to consider the plight of the accused's mother, Mrs Ellen Lee, and of his daughter Amelia Lee, and the effect the hanging would have upon them. A meeting of the Building Trades Union met and resolved to create what *The Observer* called a 'Proposed Execution Holiday.' Protests against the hanging were to no avail, and the date was fixed.

As Lee was led on to the drop at the Adelaide Gaol, he was asked, 'Is there anything you wish to say?' Alexander nodded and simply said 'Goodbye Jim,' to a prison warder. *The Advertiser* reported that as the executioner was preparing him for his doom, 'he winked at one of the officials and

---

3    Walter Robert Lee, who had served in World War I, and William Joseph
     Lee were both councillors for the West Ward of Burra.

unflinchingly walked to the gallows.' The death occurred quickly. Lee was 31 years old.

Further research on Alexander Lee led to the astonishing discovery[4] that he was the nephew of Martha Needle, who in her lifetime was known as *'The Black Widow'* and *'The Poisoner'* of the *'The Richmond Poisoning Case'*. The stories of her crimes, committed in the Colony of Victoria, were relayed across the world at the end of the 19th century and her arrest was even reported in *The New York Times*. She had killed her husband, two children and her new fiancé's brother. Martha was one of only five women hanged in Victoria, 26 years before Alexander Lee died by the same means. She was also 31 years old.

Throughout the contemporary newspaper reports were attempts to understand the tragic events and alleged motivations for Martha's crimes. There were no confessions or accusations from Martha, just a denial of her crimes and pleading of innocence.

What motivated Martha to commit these crimes and what was the evidence for her deeds? How did she get away with killing her family and another man before any suspicions were aroused? Was she a wilful poisoner and inherently evil, a 'she devil' as reported in the New Zealand newspapers? Were her crimes motivated by desperate poverty and hope to claim insurance money for her own survival, as some newspapers of the day suggested? Or was she wealthy, as other contemporary articles suggested? Were the murders crimes of passion, spurred by Martha's infatuation with her gentle fiancé of Danish

---

4    I googled Alexander Newland Lee in early 2010 and discovered commentary by Tammy Martin on the now defunct website 'Macabre Melbourne' (by Caitlin O Brien) which had a page on Martha Needle. This commentary linked the relationship between Alexander Newland Lee and Martha Needle.

descent from the Barossa Valley, Otto Juncken? One religious perspective was that other figures in Martha's life were responsible for her terrible fate, and the newspapers illuminated the discord within her family. Or was Martha criminally insane? Her lawyer and some contemporary writings posited that she had a mental illness and was unaware of her deeds. From the start, it was clear that Martha Needle's life, character and motivations would not be easy to clarify amidst the stories of the past and present media and information on her life. I was also curious to know, did Alexander Lee know his Auntie Martha and grow up with stories of her infamous deeds? Thus began my search of Martha Needle and the circumstances that led to a series of terrible deaths.

Along the journey I found some interesting twists and turns. The person who sold Martha Needle the box of poison that led to one of her victim's deaths was George Miller – the name of my great-great-grandfather who was indeed a contemporary, did live in Melbourne and was a 'clerk' at the time. I will never know if he was the same George Miller who sold Martha Needle the fatal box of poison. I also discovered that one of the descendants of Martha Needle's fiancé had found out by accident that his ancestor had been embroiled in this famous court case when coming across a book in a library that mentioned her deeds; the story of Martha's crimes had not been passed down through his family history. Perhaps most astounding were the significant achievements of the kindly Otto Juncken and the important legacy he has left Australia beyond his life with Martha Needle, given the terrible tragedies he experienced as a young man.

# 2

# Unfortunate beginnings

The 1890s was a period of economic depression in Australia, and more hangings than usual took place in the Old Melbourne Gaol. This was also the era of 'babyfarming' where children were meant to be cared for in private arrangements for small sums of money, but where many babies (some only a few weeks old) and infants were abandoned or murdered by these carers. Babyfarming was a common trade in the 1890s depression, and often occurred on a long-term basis. Both baby farmers and those that risked their children placed with them were often poor.

This was the world in which Martha Needle lived. She suffered extreme physical and sexual violence as a child and later violence from her husband, with profound conse- quences for her mental health, the safety of her children and significant others around her, and ultimately for her own life. The poverty experienced by Martha and her family was severe and the economic depression, absence of welfare and attention to the needs of children at the time contributed to their dire circumstances.

In 1894, Martha Needle was hanged in Victoria, the same year that Francis Knorr, 'the babyfarmer,' went to the gallows.

In Martha's childhood, there were few organisations or systems supporting children in need. The Victorian Neglected Children's Aid Society was established in 1894 – the same month that Martha Needle was hanged – as an interdenominational and independent society to support children who were considered neglected and destitute. Children were committed by courts to this private society which had its own homes or approved foster care homes, or parents signed over guardianship. Shortly after, the secular Victorian Society for the Prevention of Cruelty to Children was established with the aim of preventing cruelty and neglect of children. Children's courts were established in Victoria in 1906, which heard cases of child neglect and abuse, with a quarter of cases being about child neglect in 1901.

*

Murbko and North-West Bend Stations were sheep runs in 'frontier country,' at that time owned by a Scotsman, Mr Glen - the Manager of Nor-West Bend was Donald McLean who came from the Orkney Islands like Martha's mother. Nor-West Bend was situated on a lagoon and consisted of a few buildings including a hotel that doubled up as a post-office receiving only weekly communication (now known as Brenda Park Station, nine kilometres from present day Morgan), whilst Murbko[5] was further downstream on the opposite side, stretching towards Blanchetown (sixteen kilometres south east of Morgan). This region is a beautiful place of fiery limestone cliffs, river red gums, dry Mallee scrub, kangaroos, whistling kites and spectacular sunsets.

---

5    The 'Murbko Run' was established in 1860 by early settler, pastoralist and Justice of the Peace, Eardley Thomas Louis Heywood.

Large ants run furiously in all directions across the parched earth. Birdlife is abundant around the river. The distinctive call of crows pierces the sparse terrain and peaceful, monotonous afternoons. Closer to the river, ibis can be seen skimming the water's edge whilst a variety of birds swarm in and out of the gums. The river is wide and dangerous, fast flowing and often flooding, cutting off communication points in centuries past. It is an idyllic spot for holiday goers, or a prison escapee. A perfect place to hide for both Mary and Daniel 'alias Kenedy' who were on the run from authorities, but for different reasons.

*

By the time of her death at just 31 years of age, Martha had carried four surnames, but had only married once. When she was born at Murbko Station on the 9th April, 1863 in South Australia,[6] her name was registered as 'Martha Kenedy', her father was reported as 'Daniel Kenedy' and her mother as 'Mary Kenedy, formerly Newlands.'[7] Curiously, there was no one by the name of 'Kenedy' in either her biological or her step-family. Martha would also be known as 'Martha Charles' and 'Martha Foran' as she was growing up.

Martha's mother was really named 'Mary Charles' at Martha's birth, but hid her name from the authorities on Martha's birth certificate. Mary had just started a new relationship with Daniel Foran whilst she was pregnant and still married to Joseph Charles, and on the run for having abandoned her children on more than one occasion. Mary

---

6     Birth certificate of Martha Needle.
7     Newlands and Newland were used interchangeably (appeared as Newlands in Scotland): the family name became known as Newland.

had finally left her three other surviving children to take up with Foran, and may have done this for her own survival, having been abandoned by Joseph Charles and knowing that her other children would be sent to and taken care of in the Adelaide Destitute Asylum.

Mary had experienced many trials and tribulations in her young life, and it had always been one of survival. She was born Mary Newland in 1835 in Dundee, a seaport town in the county of Forfar, Scotland. At about 13 years of age she went to work at the remote Millbridge farm at Rendall, one of the Orkney Islands, north east of Scotland. The owner of the farm was Hugh Morwick,[8] a farmer with twenty acres, employing two labourers and a boy, including John Oman, 18 years, and 13 year old cow herder David Scott.[9] The Morwick's had a daughter, Elizabeth, just two years younger than Mary and three sons who had already all left the farm, the older son Hugh being a mariner who would soon go to Australia. It wasn't long before Mary, at 16 years of age, said goodbye to Mr Hugh Morwick and his wife Elizabeth, their daughter Elizabeth and the other servants. She was leaving the cold and desolate farm for her new journey to sunny South Australia.

The first step of the journey was to sail from Rendall to Plymouth, Devonshire on the opposite side of the United Kingdom. They left the wintery Plymouth dock on the ship *Caucasian* in November 1851, arriving in Port Adelaide, South Australia to full summer on 6th February 1852. At that time, Mary was 17 years of age.[10] In all, there were 17 other single women and children from Orkney on the ship. The

---

8   Also known as Marwick.
9   1851 Census, Evie and Rendall, Orkney, Scotland, District No 5. Isbister
10  The Ships List: http://www.theshipslist.com/ships/australia/
    caucasian1852.shtml

girls' decision to go to Australia was boosted by newspaper stories of eternal sunshine, abundant jobs for servants and kind and generous colonials looking for wives.

> *There is an unlimited demand for wives of all ranks, from the shepherd to the gentleman squatter, with his 1,000 head of cattle, and 20,000 sheep. The Colonists, as a body, whether emigrants or native born, make good husbands, kind, indulgent, and generous. They are all rather rough in their language to each other, but no one ever heard of a Bushman beating his wife...Young widows and orphans of small means will find themselves in reality much safer in an Australian town than in any of the great towns of Europe, better protected, and with better prospects.*
> Sidney's Emigrant Journal, 1848

The young girls were part of a plan to populate the colonies with Scottish and Irish single women and orphans, finding them employment as servants at the same time as providing future wives for the new colonists. There was not much to leave behind, as marriage prospects and jobs in Orkney were quickly disappearing due to the potato famine and land clearances. There were many Scottish families and single women emigrants from around Great Britain on the ship *Caucasian*. More than 1.7 million people left Scotland during this period.

The British Colony of South Australia, where the *Caucasian* was headed, was established in 1836 and, unlike other states of Australia, it was not a convict settlement. Its colonial founders were free-settlers and civil libertarians who had a mission to create an idyllic, morally upright society. Colonisation of the state through assisted immigration was promoted by Edward Gibbon Wakefield who created plans for its systematic colonisation when he was imprisoned in Newgate prison, London, for three years after abducting (with the help of his brother William) and marrying a 15 year old heiress, Ellen Turner, in 1826.[11] It was in Newgate prison where Wakefield was exposed to the plight of the prisoners, and he reportedly studied emigration and explored colonisation as a solution to the overcrowding and social problems of Britain — however it appears that colonisation initiatives undertaken by the Wakefields, especially in New Zealand, were largely financial ventures and morally dubious land grabs.

Wakefield's associates from his days in Newgate – Gouger and Bacon – submitted the first proposals for South Australia. Wakefield lobbied for the passing of the bill that led to the establishment of South Australia, and when it was passed he wrote the book *The New British Province of South Australia* in 1835.[12] An assisted immigration scheme for South Australia was soon established. However, there was tension between Edward Wakefield and Robert Torrens[13] who was chair of the colonisation commission for South Australia, regarding the price of land in South Australia and the

---

11   Wakefield had a sordid history of eloping with or abducting young rich girls. He had previously eloped with a ward of Chancery, Eliza Pattle (a marriage later approved through parliament as a result of lobbying the Lord Chancellor) and had two children with her (Susan and Edward Jerningham), although she had died in 1820, five days after giving birth to Jerningham, leaving him a substantial life income.

12   Graeme L. Pretty, 'Wakefield, Edward Gibbon (1796–1862)', Australian Dictionary of Biography, National Centre of Biography, Australian National University, http://adb.anu.edu.au/biography/wakefield-edward-gibbon-2763/text3921, published first in hardcopy 1967

13   Not to be confused with Torrens' son Robert Torrens who was instrumental in developing the Torrens title system for publicly registering land titles.

principle of 'concentration' of land. The Irishman, Torrens, saw emigration as a solution to reducing poverty in Ireland. The government's assisted emigration scheme was meant to be paid for by the sale of land in the new colony. Landowners were also meant to be able to use the proceeds of buying land to send out for labourers.[14] In theory, the price of land was meant to be such that labourers would have to work for some years before they could buy land. However, promoters of emigration to the state promised otherwise:

> *We therefore recommend Emigrants, wishing to live in a fine country with elbow room, and where industry is sure to be rewarded to lose no time in shipping themselves and their children to South Australia. We want no idlers – no drunkards. But steady sober men, not ashamed to live by the sweat of their brow, will be welcomed – and cannot fail to become independent in a few years.*[15]

Torrens influenced setting of the land price to be extremely low and subsequently land sales increased, demand for emigration to South Australia increased substantially and land sales eventually bottomed out. Around half of the money from the land sold went back into paying for free passage to South Australia and the colony was soon bankrupt for the first time.[16]

---

14  Atkinson & Aveling. (1987). Australians: A Historical Library: Australians 1838. Fairfax, Syme & Weldon Associates, NSW, Australia.
15  Ibid, p. 348.
16  Whalan D. Sir Robert Richard Torrens, Australian Dictionary of Biography. Wakefield later turned to the cause of establishing a colony in New Zealand and set up the Canterbury Association and New Zealand Company for this purpose. The history of the Wakefield family in New Zealand was scandalous, controversial and tragic. Edward Wakefield became a colonist in New Zealand himself, arriving in Christchurch in 1853 before moving to Wellington. There, Edward was depressed, embroiled in family conflict and

Many poor emigrants who did arrive in the Colony of South Australia were motivated by aspirations and hope, relying upon oral tales and orations on the new colony, as many were illiterate. For many, their circumstances were barely changed upon arrival in the colony, and for some they worsened. Many parents or children died either upon the long voyage over or once arrived in the new colony. Upon arrival in South Australia, immigrants were given up to three months' accommodation and two week's rations and then were left to fend for themselves.[17] Immigrants initially lived in the Adelaide Parklands in tents (where some babies were born) until they could find alternative accommodation but were eventually ejected by the Governor.[18]

Many 'free subjects' in South Australia required support with food, clothing, shelter and medical treatment as they were not fully independent settlers (and the colony was unprepared for the mass immigration). There were initially so few funds for the government hospital 'Infirmary' (no fuel, wood, water, candles, soap or beds) that Thomas Cotter, the Principal Medical Officer, announced that he could take no more patients. When the Infirmary was re-established only the 'truly destitute' would be treated free of charge and they had to see an Infirmary board member first to confirm their destitute status.[19]

Mary Newland and the other poor servant girls arrived in 1852, sixteen years after the colony was established. They

---

a failed political career as he was denied office due to his criminal record. He died in Wellington in 1862. His son Jerningham became a politician but his years were shrouded by alcoholism and disgrace for his 'relationships' with Maori women, and he died aged 41 and penniless in Ashburton's Old Men's Home.

17  Atkinson & Aveling. (1987). Op cit.
18  Ibid., p.361
19  Ibid, p. 253-353.

arrived in Port Adelaide, labelled 'Port Misery' in 1839 as it was an 'uninhabitable swamp'[20], with one of the local pubs called 'Help Me Through The Years.' The girls travelled to Emigration Square and registered at the Colonial Labour Office on King William Street, Adelaide, which was opened under the Superintendent of the Immigration Office. Having been taken over by the Immigration Agent, the Colonial Labour Office was where servants and labourers looking for employment could register and then be matched by government agents through private arrangements. Employers were required to register with the Secretary or the Immigration Agent for the service.[21]

Servant girls in the new colony had trouble finding and keeping a job as there was unexpectantly high competition for work, the problem of dubious 'masters' for these young girls, and low wages. By 1855 there were more servant girls sent to South Australia than were jobs available, leading to the establishment of local depots in every township which were to assist girls to find work.[22]

---

20   South Australian Register, 29 November 1839: T. Horton James wrote: 'The shore is an uninhabitable swamp and the few people who are living in wigwams at Port Adelaide are too busy engaged in landing boards and rolling up casks to take any notice of a party of ladies and gentlemen up to their knees in mud, trying to reach the shore ... This is Port Adelaide! Port Misery would be a better name, for nothing in any other part of the world can surpass it in everything that is wretched and inconvenient.'

21   The young girls of the Caucasian would have had to wait until the Colonial Labour Office had reopened in March 1852, for it had been temporarily closed in the city as there were plans to move it to Port Adelaide where passengers looking for work arrived. It had also just changed hands to be managed by the Immigration Agent rather than privately. It had first been established by Samuel Stocks, Esquire, businessman and Secretary of the Christchurch Sunday School (North Adelaide) who was appointed to the Destitute Board in 1852. Samuel Stocks junior, his son, had arrived in the colony in 1852 and heavily invested in the South Australian Mining Association at Burra, where many labourers were required.

22   The Domestic Servant in Colonial South Australia.
      http://www.slsa.sa.gov.au/manning/sa/social/domestic.htm

*

It wasn't long before Mary Newland and Englishman and labourer Joseph Charles found each other. Joseph had arrived three years before Mary and had come from even more dire circumstances. Joseph had arrived in Port Adelaide in 1849 on the *Indian*, travelling with two other single men and a married couple, after an eventful four-month journey. After the ship's arrival, a meeting was held where 97 emigrants from the *Indian* sought to ensure that its captain, surgeon and crew were held accountable for a range of misdemeanours, including:

> *assault, fornication, adultery, selling of ardent spirits, permitting gambling aboard the ship, smoking and drinking between decks and other crimes....on one occasion when under the influence of strong liquor, the second mate went below and declared "he would send the ship and passengers to hell."*[23]

Joseph may have been part of the alcohol fuelled mayhem as he and the two single men he travelled with had all come from the 'Old Pye' Ragged School in Westminster[24], an industrial school for boys situated in what Charles Dickens described as the 'Devil's Acre.' In Old Pye Street where the Ragged School was located, there was a house offering lessons in pickpocketing.[25] In 1855 this area was colourfully described:

---

23   Public Meeting of Emigrants by The Barque 'Indian'. South Australian Register 1 September 1849.
24   A far cry from the current prestigious Westminster private secondary school in Adelaide.
25   Kennedy, op cit.

*It is in these narrow streets, and in these close and unsalubrious lanes, courts and alleys, where squalid misery and poverty struggles with filth and wretchedness, where vice reigns unchecked and in the atmosphere of which diseases are generated and diffused.*[26]

Boys went to the industrial schools for a range of reasons: family poverty, parental imprisonment, single parenthood, the death of parents or abandonment at a time when there was no welfare. Transporting these boys to the colonies was believed to be the solution to their misery, and provision was made for their emigration.[27]

The hopes of Mary and Joseph for a better life were joined when they were married on 5th December, 1853, at Inverbrackie Cottage at Inverbrackie in the Adelaide Hills, where a small Scottish community had settled. The wedding was officiated by Reverend John Macbean *'after publication of Banns according to the forms and usages of the Church of Scotland.'* Only 18 years old Mary signed the marriage certificate with her cross to show her consent: her groom was five years her senior. The witnesses to the wedding were the Reverend's wife, Elizabeth Macbean, and Mary's friend Margaret Robertson, who also made her mark with a cross.

After their Hills marriage, Mary and Joseph soon made the long journey back to the small town of Allen's Creek, five

---

26    Cited in: Jane Kennedy, J. A short history of the Parish,.
        http://www.stmw.org/history-1.html

27    Unfortunately, circumstances were often similar in the new land, and in the late 1870s the destitute asylum and Boys Reformatory School was so full that many teenage boys were imprisoned in a reformatory hulk off Largs Bay in South Australia, the Fitzjames, in 1880. In 1883, a parliamentary inquiry into the hulk was ordered, and the 1885 inquiry report condemned conditions on board for the 62 boys and teenagers vulnerable to abuse and neglect, however it was not abandoned until 1891.

kilometres north-west of Kapunda, in the north of the colony, where copper mining was a newly emerging industry. Allen's Creek mine was established in 1847 and, by 1851, the town had fifty houses, an inn and a flour mill, and by 1856 a school was conducted from the chapel.[28]

Mary and Joseph Charles also worked at the large Anlaby station, where their daughter Ellen was born. Anlaby sheep station and homestead was north-east of Kapunda and employed a large number of servants and labourers. The station was leased by Scotsman Frederick H. Dutton in 1843 and managed by his brother Francis who would twice become Premier of South Australia. Along with Charles Hervey Bagot's son Charles Samuel, Francis Dutton was one of the finders of the first copper in the region. Irishman Charles Hervey Bagot had received land on the River Light after conducting a special land survey, which he named 'Koonunga,' and worked on together with the Dutton brothers.[29] When his son Charles Samuel and Francis Dutton found the copper, the Kapunda mine was soon established.

However, despite her parent's Church of Scotland wedding, and the Dutton's ties to the Church of Scotland, when Ellen Charles was christened at Kapunda[30] it was in the Catholic faith. The transition from 'Church of Scotland' to Catholicism may have been related to the Charles' family's poverty and any subsequent assistance received from the Catholic Church at Kapunda.[31]

---

28  Flinders Ranges Research, Allen's Creek Bethlehem Lutheran Cemetery, https://www.southaustralianhistory.com.au/allenscreek.htm

29  Bagot, Charles Hervey (1788–1880)', Australian Dictionary of Biography, National Centre of Biography, Australian National University, http://adb.anu.edu.au/biography/bagot-charles-hervey-1730/text1903, published first in hardcopy 1966. Also, Flinders Ranges Research, Koonunga District, https://www.southaustralianhistory.com.au/koonunga.htm

30  Recorded christening 2nd July 1861 at 'Charles Melville Summit Convent', Kapunda. Source: Family history research records by Tammy Martin. There is little record of this place or convent.

*

Over the first eight years of their marriage, Mary and Joseph had a number of children including William in 1854, Mary in 1856, Ellen in 1859, and Dinah in 1861. A month after their youngest daughter Dinah was born, Joseph deserted Mary and their four children, leaving them with only £7. Without any financial support, Mary had few options but to apply for relief from the Destitute Board through the local court house. It was just one example of many where she would come in contact with authorities.[32] Her dire circumstances could be read by anyone purchasing a copy of Adelaide's main daily newspaper:

### Destitute Board

*Thursday, June 13th [1861] Application from Country Districts*

*Kapunda – Mr J. S. Browne, S.M. [Special Magistrate], on behalf of Mary Charles, whose husband deserted her about a month since, leaving her 7l,[33] and stating that it was not his intention to return. Two rations were granted, and a warrant issued for the apprehension of her husband.*

*The South Australian Advertiser, 15th June 1861*

---

31  This is the parish linked to the excommunication of Saint Mary MacKillop. In early 1870, the Josephite nuns heard allegations that Father Keating from the Kapunda church was sexually abusing children, which was duly reported. Keating eventually got sent back to Ireland and Father Horan's vengeance upon the Josephites (Sisters of St Joseph of the Sacred Heart, headed by Mother Mary MacKillop, now Saint Mary of the Cross), would cause problems for the order and excommunication for MacKillop.

32  A female with the surname Newland was with a son in the Destitute Asylum in 1855, and this may have been Mary using her maiden name.

33  7 pounds

There were no signs of Joseph having returned by April 1862 when 11 month old Dinah died from dysentery, probably due to lack of access to clean water, as Kapunda was notorious for problems with its water supply. Dinah was buried in the Kapunda Public Cemetery on the Clare Road. Mary stated that she was a widow on her baby's death certificate, although there is no record of her husband Joseph's death, and the authorities later believed that Joseph was alive and living under an alias. Mary likely knew that it would be difficult to locate Joseph to obtain a divorce and that if the authorities believed that she was a widow it would pave the way to marry again.

The police were sure that Joseph was still alive as in 1863 and 1864, arrest warrants were out for both Mary and Joseph for deserting their children at Kapunda on the 9th November, 1862, as advertised in the SA *Police Gazette*. By November 1862 when she deserted her children, Mary was four months pregnant. When Martha was born in April 1863, Mary claimed that she was Joseph Charles's baby. The reconciliation with Joseph (if it occurred) did not last long. During her pregnancy, Mary found another suitor, the Irishman Daniel Foran. He would have a profound impact on Martha's life and his story helps to understand what would become the tragedy of her life.

It may have been at the local Catholic Church where Mary had met Daniel, a shepherd on the large Murbko station. Daniel had led a colourful life before winding up at the remote station. He was 16 years old when he signed up for the British Army in his home town of Caherconlish, Limerick, where he lived in a small rented house with his mother, also Mary. When Daniel made his mark to sign up to the service, the army recorded that Daniel was 5 foot 6 inches tall, with a fresh complexion, light brown hair and hazel eyes. Daniel would have been eager to join the British 'redcoats' for travel and adventure, as well as a means of survival, as there were few prospects in Ireland.

Shortly after, in 1855 Daniel sailed into Melbourne in the Colony of Victoria on the ship *Windsor* with 400 fellow rank and file soldiers from the $2^{nd}/40^{th}$ Regiment of Foot (Second Somersetshire). Many years earlier, the famous regiment had served in the battle at Waterloo. It was now deployed on Garrison Duty in Australia, largely as convict guards. It had been involved in the brutal battle of the Eureka stockade on the Victorian goldfields just prior to Daniel and other soldiers boosting their numbers in Australia.

Like other lowly ranked privates in the army, Daniel was discouraged from marrying due to his low salary. Desertion was a chronic problem for the British army in Australia, so much so that the topic of desertion was specifically addressed by the Governor of Victoria during one speech to the regiment. This provided little discouragement as Daniel received a considerable number of lashes for deserting the regiment on three occasions.

The first escape was in 1855 with two fellow soldiers, and the trio 'took part of their regimental necessities with them.' Foran was shortly recaptured before deserting again in 1855. The price paid for his various escapes included having a 'D' for 'Deserter' tattooed under his left arm on at least two occasions. Even after his 1855 recapture, Foran did not stay out of trouble. He was at the Lightning Hotel in Bourke Street, Melbourne in 1856 when he saw a familiar face following him out of the hotel – twenty year old Irishman John Donovan, *'a strong man of repulsive appearance'* who beckoned him into a house, but Daniel refused. A fight soon ensued and witnesses in the later court case reported that they heard Daniel screaming as he was knelt upon by Donovan near the Adam and Eve public house on Little Collins Street. There may have been a fight with Donovan who would have feared being reported by Foran. Donovan was at that time an escapee of the 40th Regiment who had been at Bendigo and was not only running away from the police and the regiment: there was a £2 reward for any member of the general public who captured deserters (just down from £10). Donovan was sentenced to six months hard labour for desertion, although he made his final escape one month later at Geelong.

Perhaps inspired by Donovan, Foran escaped the Regiment in 1857 on the goldfields at Sandhurst (Bendigo) but was again recaptured and sentenced to four years' jail. His subsequent and final escape in September 1861 was from the outer yard of the Central Gaol in Melbourne, where he was employed as a groom to the Governor of the Gaol. He was under the charge of a warder when he escaped. He was described as follows: 21 years, 5 foot 6 inches, fresh complexion, brown hair, blue eyes, born Limerick, deserted at Melbourne on 14th September 1861, brand 'D' under left arm. The escape was reported in newspapers as far away as the Colony of Queensland and authorities supposed that Foran would '*endeavour to remove to New Zealand.*' If caught, punishment for Foran on the fourth occasion of desertion from the British Army, whilst serving a jail term, would have been severe. Daniel headed for South Australia where many escaped criminals ended up, and he quickly found work at Murbko station. Both running from the law, Mary and Daniel adopted the name 'Ken[n]edy,' borrowing the name from a fellow escapee of Daniel from a previous escape.

\*

Exactly a year after Martha Needle's birth on 9[th] April 1863, the warrant was still outstanding in the *Police Gazette* for Mary and Joseph Charles' desertion of their children. By this time there were only two children left, as poor William Charles died from whooping cough in January 1864 in the Royal Adelaide Hospital. He was ten years of age and his runaway parents were not recorded on the registration of his death. Siblings Mary and Ellen Charles were sent to the Destitute Asylum.[34]

Mary Kennedy had started a new life and family on the West Coast of South Australia, including Fowler's Bay (916 kilometres from Adelaide) and Lake Hamilton (694 kilometres from Adelaide). By the time Martha was three years old she was living at Lake Hamilton station on the Eyre Peninsula where Daniel Kennedy continued as a shepherd. This was even more remote than Murbko. Lake Hamilton is in stony, desolate pastoral country where it took over two weeks for the mail to travel from Adelaide. At the time the 'Kennedys' were living there, the pastoral run was owned by Mr Price Maurice whose interests on the Eyre Peninsula included 97,000 sheep to be shorn each year. It was at Lake Hamilton on the 13th April 1866 that Martha's half-brother, Daniel Foran junior was born.

---

34   However, Mary Charles did not want to completely abandon her other children. In March 1864, 'Mary Kennedy' of Port Lincoln wrote to the Destitute Asylum saying that if her two nieces by the name of Charles were sent to her free of charge, she would look after them. There was a recommendation that they be sent. However, it appears that Mary and Ellen Charles remained in the Destitute Asylum. By 1870, Mary Charles jnr, aged 13 ½ years old, was boarded out from the Destitute Asylum as a servant, with Mr Cox at Enfield.   She was re-admitted to the asylum in October 1870 having returned from service, not being able to work due to a 'bad knee', and she left shortly after to go to school. She lists only having a sister (Ellen) in the colony.

The family also lived at Bramfield, near Elliston, Little Swamp and Proper Bay, near Port Lincoln, still on the West Coast of South Australia. Bridging the isolation of the West Coast for Mary was the strong Scottish community of Port Lincoln, which proudly kept their cultural traditions and love of dance. This community included famous explorer John McDouall Stuart, whose explorations paved the way of the Stuart Highway from Adelaide to Darwin, and Irish poet Thomas (Tom) Black who lived on the shores of Proper Bay. The 'Kennedys' attended the Anglican church in Port Lincoln and, at one time, Daniel worked for the warden of the St Thomas's Church, Mr Edward Bartlett. Daniel and the family changed their name back to 'Foran' when he married Mary on March 15th 1870.[35] However, Daniel was now using the alias 'David' Foran. The next month, seven year old Martha was baptised with the surname Foran when the family were living in Lake Hamilton. Shortly after this, they moved to Bramfield, near Elliston.

From this time, the Foran family was plagued with a set of tragedies and poor health. Seven months after Mary and Daniel's marriage, twins John and Margaret Foran were born, on 27th October 1870 at Bramfield, however Margaret died. When Mary went to the Royal Adelaide Hospital for two months in 1873 due to a leg ulcer it was likely to be serious. Ten year old Martha was left to look after her brothers who were seven and three years old. The following year the Foran family moved back to Adelaide, settling in Bowden and North Adelaide, and Mary was again pregnant. That year Martha was hospitalised twice for purulent ophthalmia, a condition where the eyes are swollen and kept constantly closed, caused

---

35 Marriage certificate states May Charles.

by poor hygiene and living in cold and damp conditions – although one explanation is that this is 'usually of gonorrhoeal origin,' and a bacterial infection. It was in the Destitute Asylum of Adelaide and other care institutions that ophthalmia, more commonly known as 'blight', was rife, and in severe cases it sent children and adults blind.[36]

It seems that the Foran children were often left at home to fend for themselves. Mary was in and out of jail and received fines for drunken behaviour and obscene language. She was charged on 11th January 1875, 31st March 1875 and on 3rd April 1875 for drunkenness, insulting behaviour and 'uttering foul words.' She was heavily pregnant at the time and on 7th April 1875, two days before Martha's 12th birthday, her new baby George was born and died after just one hour in the Adelaide hospital. He was buried in the West Terrace Cemetery on the 9th April 1875.

The following month, when living in Sussex Street, North Adelaide, Martha was again hospitalised for purulent conjunctivitis and her brother Daniel was hospitalised for the same condition. In November, for just over one month, their mother Mary went to hospital for her leg ulcer. In December 1875, whilst her mother was in hospital, Martha Charles came to the attention of a neighbour as she could be heard crying out. The situation in the household was finally revealed.

---

36   Ball, C, Seeing clearly at the Destitute Asylum – an eyebath, September 20th, 2016. https://migration.history.sa.gov.au/blog/seeing-clearly-at-the-destitute-asylum-an-eyebath/

# 3

# Child Witness

Martha's mother was in hospital with a bad leg when her Dada troubled her. In Port Lincoln there may have been no point screaming as there may have been no neighbours nearby but this time, in North Adelaide in the city, she screamed as loud as she could. We know from the subsequent court case that Martha's screams had alerted a neighbour:

'Dada, don't hurt me,' she cried. Danny ran out of the room.

Mrs Higgins who lived next door to us in Sussex Street walked past and hearing the child's terrified screams she looked through the window. She was shocked to see Mr Foran on top of the poor girl. She soon banged on the pane. She made the two steps towards the door of the house and opened it without hesitation.

'Get off that poor child' she yelled. Mr Foran was surprised and moved away.

'Come to me, Martha,' Mrs Higgins said. Martha ran to Mrs Higgins, crying. Her ear was cut and bleeding. 'What is the matter?' asked Mrs Higgins. 'How did you cut your ear?'

'You know very well what is the matter with me,' Martha said angrily.

Mrs Higgins turned to Daniel Foran. 'You should be ashamed of yourself. I'm going to fetch for the police.'

Martha followed Mrs Higgins next door, and they called for the policeman. When the policeman came, he spoke to Martha kindly. He told her that she would have to answer questions in the Adelaide courthouse. Martha stayed at Mrs Higgins's until her mother got out of the Adelaide hospital. When Mrs Foran came back from the hospital, Mrs Higgins spoke to her mother. 'That child should never be left alone in the house with Daniel. He can't be trusted with his stepdaughter.'

But Martha went home when her mother came back. The heavily pregnant Mary confronted Daniel about the abuse. It was not long before Mary was back in the Adelaide hospital with bruises all over her body.

Martha was given the opportunity to speak at the Court about Daniel Foran's treatment of her, something that she would be deprived of as an adult. But when the court day arrived, Martha was too scared or ashamed to say much. When they got to the Adelaide courthouse, it was Danny who was the first witness to speak. He was nine years old. Mr Wadey was the lawyer for the prosecution.

'Where did you sleep?' asked Mr Wadey.

'We slept in the bedroom, Mama, Dada, Martha, John and myself. Dada slept on the couch' said Danny. He said that he saw his Dada interfere with Martha a number of times.

Daniel senior was in the dock. Martha looked down as Mr Wadey began questioning her.

'Is what Danny saying true?' he asked. She nodded, too afraid to say anything. 'Is it true, Martha?' he repeated.

'Yes sir.'

Yet when it was Daniel senior's turn, he swore that he never touched Martha.

Daniel Foran was charged with indecently assaulting his 12 year old step-daughter on March 10th 1876 and given a sentence of two years' hard labour. He was received by the Adelaide Gaol on 5th April, 1876. Foran was sentenced by Judge Stow, who had just been appointed to the Supreme Court of South Australia. The description of Foran by the Gaol authorities indicates that the 'D' branding of the British Army for being a deserter had been replaced by a crucifix, although now Foran, an Irish Catholic, had stated to the authorities that he was 'Church of England' and employed as a 'Gossamist.' The case led to an article in the South Australian *Register* where Foran's abuse was associated with 'overcrowding' in houses for the poor. It appears from the article below that the issue of the child's consent may have been raised in the court case, given the direction by the Judge that this suggestion be dismissed and the power of the step-father over her be taken into account. It was not until 1885 that the age of sexual consent was raised from 13 to 16 years of age,[37] following the Criminal Law Consolidation Amendment Act, which suffragist Mary Lee had advocated for. Notably, reporting on the Foran case referred to Martha as 13 years of age, although she was still 12 years of age.

*Overcrowding in Houses – Editorial*

*The case of Daniel Foran, who was tried at the late sittings of the Supreme Court, brings to light the existence of a state of things in this city which is a dark blot upon our boasted civilization and morality. The details are not such as we care to dwell upon, but it is at times desirable that the existence*

---

37   Girls could also be forced to marry at a very young age. Mrs Elizabeth Scott was the first woman hanged in Victoria (on 11th November, 1863) for conspiring with her alleged lover and another man to kill her husband (although she was not nearby). Her husband was a much older violent alcoholic man whom she had been forced to marry when she was just 13 years old. (Source: Kirkwood, 2006).

*of an evil should be made public, in order that it may not be possible to plead ignorance as an excuse for neglecting to make any attempt to remove it. Early in December last Daniel Foran committed an indecent assault on Martha Charles, a girl thirteen years of age, and his stepdaughter. The family lived in a two-roomed house situated in Lower North Adelaide. One room was used as a sitting-room and kitchen; the other as a bedroom. Besides Foran, his wife, their two children— both boys, aged respectively ten and six — and the stepdaughter, on whom the crime was committed, lived in the house. The mother and the two boys lay on a bed, the father slept on a sofa alongside the bed, and the daughter slept at the foot of her mother's bed. It may therefore be said that they all slept in one bed. His Honor said in sentencing the prisoner to the full term of imprisonment that the law permits that the contention that the child was not the prisoner's own offspring would be an idle one. The girl's mother was his wife; the girl was but three years old when he married; she had been under his influence; she had been the playmate and companion of his own children, and had been brought up under his influence. Mr. Justice Stow further said that even if the Jury thought for one moment that the evidence showed the slightest sign of consent on the part of the girl — who gave her evidence fairly and modestly— it would not in his mind amount to more than a submission produced from the habit of obedience and the influence which the prisoner had acquired over her; and such a submission would not amount to a consent sufficient to exonerate prisoner from guilt.*

*The Register, 4<sup>th</sup> April 1876*

Just over a year later, the South Australian *Police Gazette* 22<sup>nd</sup> August 1877 reported that Daniel Foran was due for freedom the following day, although he had not served his full two year term.

*

Whilst many, particularly women and children, were battling in the new colony, especially those such as Martha who were born into dire circumstances, the world was on the brink of progressive change for women. Unfortunately, this was to be too late for Martha. Two Scotswomen were striving to improve the situation of poor women and children: Catherine Helen Spence and Mary MacKillop. The celebrated South Australian Catherine Helen Spence was a regular contributor to *The Register* newspaper, and a close friend of the editor and possible contributor to editorials such as the one above. She often assumed the identity of her brother in order not to miss journalistic writing assignments. Spence was a governess and teacher, journalist (the first female professional journalist), author (the first female author to write a book about Australia), suffragist (along with Irishwoman Mary Lee, helping South Australia to become one of the first places in the world to give women the vote), Unitarian preacher (the colony's first female preacher), social and political reformer, the first female political candidate, lecturer and public speaker. Spence had arrived in South Australia with her family as a 14 year old in 1839. She was red-headed, short, with a Scottish accent, a strong sense of self-belief and humour.

Spence never married (rejecting two proposals as a teenager and young adult) or had children, although she raised three families of orphaned children, including her sister's children, and cared for her mother. In particular, Spence was an advocate for the education of girls and women's working conditions.

Whilst education was compulsory, it was not free until 1875 in South Australia, so children like Martha had few alternatives but to work from a young age. Compulsory education that was not free created heavy burdens for impoverished families, and in the view of Catherine Helen Spence, a 'caste system' between the fee payers and non-fee payers[38]. It was also not until 1879 that the first government secondary school for girls, The Advanced School for Girls, was established in South Australia by Spence.

Amongst Spence's other achievements was being a founder of the Boarding Out Society in 1872, the first foster scheme for children in South Australia aimed at getting children out of institutions and reformatories, which was imitated throughout Australia and New Zealand. Spence was appointed to the State Children's Council (in 1887) and the Destitute Board (in 1897). In 1893 at the age of 68 she lectured throughout the United States (Chicago's World Fair and Congress of Women) and Canada, Switzerland and the United Kingdom on 'effective voting.' Spence was a co-founder (with Caroline Emily Clark) of the Adelaide Children's Court in 1890, first recognised legally in 1895 (a world first), although had been a recommendation of the Way Commission's Destitute Act Commission Report in 1885. This juvenile court influenced court systems in other jurisdictions of Australia and overseas, including England.

A focus of inquiry of the Way Commission was the Fitzjames ship, a leaky and rotting reformatory hulk moored off Largs Bay in South Australia where boys and adolescents were kept. In the late 1870s, the Destitute Asylum and Boys Reformatory School was so full that many boys were

---

38    Magarey, S with Wall B, Lyons, M & Beams, M, (2005). Ever yours, C. H.
      Spence, Wakefield Press.

imprisoned for years in this reformatory hulk without going ashore. In 1883, a parliamentary inquiry into the hulk was ordered, and the Way Commission's Destitute Act Commission Report in 1885 condemned conditions on board for the 62 boys and teenagers vulnerable to abuse and neglect, and recommended that the institutionalisation of children be a last resort. However, the Fitzjames was not abandoned until 1891. Hundreds of boys, some having committed petty crime, some more serious, and others simply poor or with abusive parents, were imprisoned on this ship between 1880 and 1891 under the supervision of a known paedophile, or in the company of an older boy who was a known rapist.[39]

A contemporary of Catherine Helen Spence was Saint Mary MacKillop who was born in Melbourne in 1842, the eldest of eight children. Like Spence, she had Scottish heritage (both parents migrating from Scotland). Also similar to Spence, she began her professional life as a governess, later helping to found the Sisters of St Joseph of the Sacred Heart in 1866 (the Josephites), dedicated to the education of poor children and establishing a number of schools around South Australia from the 1860s. She lived on the corner of William and Queen Street, Norwood after her excommunication from the Catholic Church in 1871, when she was wrongly accused by Bishop Sheil of inciting 'the sisters to disobedience and defiance' and many of the Josephite schools were subsequently closed. MacKillop was exonerated five months later, just before Sheil's death in 1872. The excommunication was associated with MacKillop uncovering and making a complaint in 1871 about the sexual abuse of children by

---

39   The Fitzjames: SA's floating prison for wayward teens, The Advertiser, 3rd
     May 2017. http://www.adelaidenow.com.au/news/special-features/in-depth/
     the-fitzjames-sas-floating-prison-for-wayward-teens/news-story/
     0ec11349685e6ed09ec1152f0192300a

Father Keating and others at Kapunda (with the Vicar General taking action and sending Keating back to Ireland). Kapunda priest Father Horan, one of these priests, now worked with Bishop Sheil and wreaked revenge on MacKillop and the Josephites, changing their rules to break them up, which MacKillop refused to comply with.[40]

Shortly after being exonerated, MacKillop travelled to Rome to have the rules of the Order approved, and when she returned she became Superior-General of the Order. On the grounds of St Ignatius (Queen Street) the Order established a Women's Refuge where women ex-prisoners, unmarried mothers and homeless women lived and were taught to be self-supporting. An orphanage was also created along with a home for older women. The Order was established throughout Australia and in New Zealand where she spent three years. Later in 1883, Bishop Reynolds of Adelaide attempted to destroy the Josephites and Mary as their head as she advocated for a more centralised, equalitarian and less hierarchical organisation: she was exiled and removed as Superior-General of the Order. The Josephites transferred its headquarters to Sydney and Mary MacKillop was eventually reinstated as Superior-General. She was beautified by the Pope in 1995 and became Australia's first Saint in 2010, and the first Saint ever to have been excommunicated from the Catholic Church.

*

Martha Needle briefly went to Mrs Beresford's place at North Adelaide probably to work as a general servant[41] and then

---

40    ABC. (2010). MacKillop banished after uncovering sex abuse.
      http://www.abc.net.au/news/2010-09-25/mackillop-banished-after-
      uncovering-sex-abuse/2273940

became a domestic servant for the Drew family when she was 12 years old in 1875, just a bit younger than her mother had been when she moved from Dundee to the Orkneys in Scotland. Mrs Drew of Dale Street, Port Adelaide, had been looking for a servant for some time, and to attract potential candidates she advertised that there was 'only two in the family.' Mrs Drew, who invited applicants to write to her at Dale Street, had a boy and girl just younger than Martha.

In her job as a domestic servant for Mrs Drew, Martha would have encountered many people and she was later described as charming, sociable, affable and obliging. Cornishman Mr Francis Drew was the Wharfinger at Simpson and then Queen's wharf, the main wharf of Port Adelaide, managing goods received, tide tables and the ramps used to repair and launch ships. He was also a sail master and had a lodging house at Port Bridge (Glanville). There were lots of people to meet as Port Adelaide was a hive of activity at this time, a busy harbour with railway lines, many hotels operating and buildings in the process of being built. There were many rowdy sailors and wharfies from all parts of the world hanging about the Port and its many saloons.

Just after Martha moved to Dale Street her mother had gone to jail again for two months for 'being drunk' and leaving her brothers Danny, ten years old (born April 1866) and John, still just five years old (born October 1870) at home alone with little means of support other than public charity. Her brothers were both sent to the Industrial School for boys at Magill in 1876, until they were 12 years old.[42] A part of this school was set aside as The Boys Reformatory, but in

---

41 In 1879, Mrs Beresford of North Adelaide was advertising in an Adelaide newspaper for a 'general servant'.
42 South Australia Chronicle and Weekly Mail, 15th July 1876.

1880, the boys at the Reformatory were sent to the Fitzjames Reformatory hulk, moored off Largs Bay.[43]

It seems that Daniel Foran junior had left the Industrial School by 1879 and had escaped being sent to the Fitzjames as, when he was 13, he was reported missing at Port Lincoln, and described in the *Police Gazette* as being tall for his age, with light hair, fair complexion and blue eyes. By the age of 14, in December 1880, Daniel junior was working on an oyster boat at Port Lincoln as a labourer, and was described as 'fair complexion, dark brown hair, dark hazel eyes, stoops.'[44] He had gone missing and was found again.

Martha and her older sisters, Mary and Ellen, wrote to one another, even though they had not grown up together for the most part. Mary made sure Martha knew who her sisters were. Mary and Ellen both married and lived in the north of the colony, near where they had spent their early years. At 17 years of age, Mary Charles junior married James Henry Hall in 1874. Ellen Charles married aged 21 years, to Joseph Lee, in 1880. As was a common tradition, four of Ellen's twelve children carried either the first name or surname of one of her parents, including Alexander Newland Lee.

It appears that Joseph Charles was not in touch with Martha or his other children at this time. *The Register* of 18th October 1879 reported on a man named Joseph Charles who was walking from Port Augusta to Adelaide and fell ill near Allen's Creek, where he rested in an isolated hut for three days before finally being found and sent to Kapunda Hospital by a Dr Blood. This may well have been Martha's long lost father, for he knew Allen's Creek well, it being the first place he had settled with Mary Foran.

---

43   Find and Connect, Boys Reformatory Magill,
     https://www.findandconnect.gov.au/guide/sa/SE01217
44   The South Australian Police Gazette, December 15, 1880.

# 4

# From Port Adelaide to Richmond

When Martha was 16 years of age she met a handsome, strong man named Henry Needle who was a carpenter at Port Adelaide. He was described as 'a capable workman, of good physique, and well-liked by his acquaintances and friends.' He was born in Plymouth, England, and came to South Australia with his family as a child. He came from a respectable family, well established in the Port, with the family home at Heath Street, Port Adelaide (Birkenhead). Henry's father Thomas and brothers were local carpenters at the Port, whilst his sister became head milliner at Messrs. Jones Brothers drapery establishment on St Vincent's Street, Port Adelaide.

Martha adored Henry, or Harry as he was commonly known, and she was eager to marry him. When she was 18, Martha was 'with child', but not yet married. Henry soon proposed, and she may have felt lucky as there would have been many girls who were pregnant whose suitors had abandoned them. A contemporary newspaper had reported on Sarah White, a single woman and innkeeper in North Adelaide who had died taking 'bitter apple', a kind of poison, trying to abort her baby.

Martha moved from the Port back with her family in Sussex Street, North Adelaide before she got married. Henry moved to nearby Hackney, within walking distance of Martha. Martha started making wedding preparations, carefully selecting the church. Her local priest may have refused to marry them as she was six months pregnant, which would have been difficult to hide.

One month after her 19$^{th}$ birthday, on 15$^{th}$ May 1882, Martha was married to Henry, aged 22 years, at the beautiful Christ Church (Anglican), on Montefiore Hill in North Adelaide. The witnesses at the wedding were Eliza Louisa Martin, her close friend, who lived in a cottage on the east side of Sussex Street, North Adelaide, near Martha's childhood residence, and Eliza's husband Sidney Martin, who was a painter and Grand Sentinel in the Independent Order of Good Templars, Grand Lodge. Henry soon became part of the Lodge and the four of them were the best of friends.

After the wedding, Henry and Martha went on a honeymoon straight away to a place where they could have their baby without any questions being asked. They departed on the ship 'Leura' for Sydney via Melbourne, arriving on 24$^{th}$ May 1882. Two months later, on 4 August, their child Mabel Hannah Needle was born in Sydney. The newlyweds spent around ten months in Sydney but when work ran out for Henry they returned to live in Port Adelaide.

It was not long after arriving back when Henry headed off again to Victoria to find work to support his new family. This was not a fortuitous time to be a carpenter or working in the building industry. Economic recession had set in around 1884, and between 1885 and 1890 the Colony of South Australia lost more people to emigration than it gained from immigration. Many people were leaving Adelaide for Melbourne, a bustling city of new construction. The temperance movement was at its peak and its alcohol-free coffee palaces dominated Melbourne's skyline. Martha's friend Eliza and her husband Sidney had already moved to Melbourne. Henry soon followed, arriving in Melbourne on his own in 1883, but Martha stayed in Adelaide to give birth to her second child Elsie, born in Port Adelaide, on the 6th October 1884. Elsie was the image of her father, with dark straight hair and light coloured eyes. Henry stayed at Mrs Hannah Tutt's restaurant and boarding house for three months at 153 Bridge Road, Richmond. When Martha moved to Melbourne, she lived at the Nicholson boarding house – where she would encounter fellow emigrants from South Australia, such as the Juncken brothers – before the Needles soon found a residence at 19 Wellington Street, Richmond. There Martha soon befriended her neighbours, Mr and Mrs Robinson.

Martha became connected to the social circle in Richmond through the Church, dances and social visits, whilst Henry was involved in the Odd Fellows Lodge with his friend Sidney Martin. Whilst 'everybody liked Harry', he was less sociable than Martha. Henry was jealous of the boarders and some of Martha's new friends in Melbourne. Sometimes he would get suspicious and ask where she'd been and who she was with. He would get very angry and sometimes hit her. It wasn't financially easy for the young couple in Melbourne as work soon ran out for Henry. Martha had started to keep boarders to help their family out. But sometimes the boarders were out of work and the entire household was waiting for the money to come in. The more money trouble there was, the angrier Henry would be, and then Martha had to be especially careful with the boarders lest she arouse the slightest suspicions. Eventually, Henry sought work in Sydney again whilst Martha stayed in Melbourne keeping boarders.

The worst period came in Christmas 1885 when their eldest child Mabel became ill. Henry was still in Sydney looking for work. Three days after Christmas, Mabel died and 'went to rest.' She was three years old. The doctor suspected that the child had died from a brain tumour. The Needles couldn't afford a grave, so poor Mabel was buried in a mass grave with 11 other children on 29th December, 1885. Many other little children in Melbourne had died of tuberculosis around this time.

Martha was said to be overcome with grief over the death of her child and would explain that her daughter 'just seemed to fade.' Henry came back from Sydney. They eventually scraped some money together to notify their extended friends and relatives in Adelaide of Mabel's death via a newspaper entry six weeks after the fact.

*NEEDLE—On the 28th December, at her parents' residence, 19, Wellington-street, Richmond, Melbourne, of tumour on the brain, Mabel Hannah, eldest beloved daughter of Henry and Martha Needle, aged 3 years and 7 weeks. Dear little Mabel has gone to rest.*

*The Advertiser, 3rd February 1886*

Martha became pregnant again as soon as Henry was back and on 14th September 1886, Martha gave birth to another daughter in Richmond, whom she named May. May looked like the Scottish side of the family and had fair curly hair like Martha.

Around this time, the Needle family moved frequently around Richmond. It was hard for the family to pay the rent and make ends meet, and their housing was insecure despite them still keeping boarders to help them pay the rent and living expenses. The family had moved three times in one year: from Wellington Street where they were in February

1886 to Cremorne Street, before moving to 110 Cubitt Street, Richmond, where they were living when May was born in September 1886, and later to 134 Cubitt Street.

One day Henry came home from work and Martha was talking to one of their borders who was out of work. Henry called Martha to their room, and started yelling at her. He hit Martha with a plank of wood. Terrified, she went to visit her friend Eliza.

Henry suddenly became extremely ill in 1889 and Martha called lodge Doctor Hodgson to their house. Martha had made chicken broth and jelly, which Henry would not eat. The Doctor urged Henry to eat, but he waved the meal away, causing the Doctor to remark that he was a very obstinate man for refusing to eat. Henry was seriously worried about his health and what would become of his family if he died. Elsie was nearly five years old and May was almost three, and Martha had no real means to support the family. Henry became worse over the next three weeks.[45]

Henry died on 4th October, 1889, and Dr Hodgson declared the cause of death to be 'sub-acute hepatitis and persistent vomiting. Enteric fever and exhaustion in not taking nourishment.' The Doctor had been exasperated with his patient, whose condition had lasted three weeks. There was no suspicion of poisoning, although earlier in the same year Louisa Collins had become the last woman to be hanged in the Colony of New South Wales for murdering her violent husband by poison.[46]

Henry was buried at the Kew Cemetery three days after his death. A curious note beside his death registration remarks

45   The Register, 20th June 1894
46   Overington, C. (2014). Last woman hanged: The terrible true story of Louise Collins. Harper Collins Publishers. Sydney.

'Cre 22$^{nd}$ Oct 1889'.[47] We know cremation of Henry's body did not occur, as Henry's body was subsequently dug up.

Destitute, and before the funeral and burial of her husband, Martha went to collect the insurance money the day after Henry died to have money for food and lodging. The couple had been able to fund an insurance premium: in the colonies the working poor were encouraged to belong to lodge or benefit societies in the event of illness or accidents. For example, Thomas Cotter, Principal Medical Officer at the Destitute Asylum in Adelaide, had lobbied the working classes to organise and establish private insurance funds for themselves (benefit funds).

Martha may have been worried that even though Henry had insurance, he did not write a will. Martha was told that she could not have the insurance money without a will, and that she would have to go through the court system in order to obtain funds. A month later, the case was heard, on 8$^{th}$ November, 1889, in the Supreme Court of the Colony of Victoria. The property of Henry was granted to The Trustees Executors and Agency Company Ltd of 37 Queen Street, Melbourne. The Managing Director of the Company, William Templeton, was granted administration of the estate on behalf of Martha Needle. The estate amounted to £209 and ten shillings, and included: an Australian Widow Fund Life Society insurance of £200, clothing worth £1 five shillings, an old Waterbury watch (an inexpensive pocket watch) worth five shillings and carpenters' tools worth £8. The statement of assets and liabilities noted that 'the deceased was not possessed of any landed property held under lease or license

---

47   It has been claimed that cremations for non-Indigenous Victorians did not
     occur in Victoria until 1903, however some cremations occurred from 1895
     when the first European was cremated. History of Cremation:
     http://www.ayton.id.au/gary/History/H_cremation.htm

from the Crown.' The executors for the estate granted Martha £60 of the insurance, with the remaining £120 saved for each surviving child.

Around this time Martha had studio photograph shots of herself taken, along with May and Elsie. Photographic portraiture was popular at the time. Martha had hitherto not been able to afford this. The full-length photograph of Martha shows her to be a handsome woman with fair, short curly hair, large deep set eyes, a straight nose and strong chin. Her look is hesitant due to her little frown and the way in which her left side turns slightly towards the photographer. She is dressed in the latest 19th century refinery which accentuated her slight figure. Martha wears a hat on top of her tight curls, a large silk scarf around her neck, a dress comprised of a fitted sealette velvet jacket and large floor-length ruffled skirt, with a shiny shoe peeping out from underneath her skirts. Curiously, she is carrying an umbrella. Her shoes are not done up, suggesting that Martha borrowed the clothes from the photographer's studio, as was done at the time. Appearance was especially important in this Victorian age, as it could determine one's access to public buildings such as libraries. In the photograph, Martha looked far from someone who had come from and was in the most destitute of circumstances.

*

Martha, with Elsie and May to raise alone and without any financial means, travelled back to South Australia but found she could hardly hope to receive help from her family. Her Mama was hawking (peddling goods by calling out) and living at Hilton and still getting in trouble for 'being drunk and using indecent language.' During Martha's visit, her mother was fined at the Adelaide Police Court and twice sent to the Adelaide Gaol (in May and June 1889).

The following June 1890, Mary, along with a man named Frank Brogan, was once again charged at the Adelaide Police Court, and fined £2, for being drunk and using indecent language. Fifty-three year old Mary again went to the Gaol. Upon leaving gaol, Mary was admitted to the Destitute Asylum in August 1890. Upon entry to the Destitute Asylum it was necessary to prove 'destitution' and that one could not be supported by any husband or family members. Mary stated that she had not lived with her husband Daniel Foran for eight years. She also stated that she had five children, including Mary Hall at Hoyleton, Ellen Lee, married with six children at Marrabel, Martha, 26 years old widow with two children, living at Port Adelaide, John 19 years old (she says 'not known where' – although he appeared to live at Hilton his entire adult life) and Daniel junior, 23 years old, at Streaky Bay ('not seen for 13 years-since he entered the Industrial School'). Martha was likely staying with her in-laws at Port Adelaide at the time, although she had very little contact with them.[48] Mary was recommended to the asylum by Dr A. S. Patterson. Upon admission it states she was, 'discharged from the Adelaide Gaol in a weak and debilitated condition and Dr Pattinson recommends her for admission here and expresses the opinion that she is not able to earn a living at present. Her family is in poor circumstances.'

Mary stayed in the Destitute Asylum for around six weeks. It was likely she had bumped into her estranged husband as in July 1890, Daniel Foran, who was living in Crafers in the Adelaide Hills, had also been admitted. He states that he was

48   The Register, 18th June 1894

at first a soldier then a cook, and that he supposed his wife Mary was at Hilton. He mentions his two sons, Daniel 24 years and John, 19 years old, whom he had not seen for nine years and five years respectively. He was also referred to the asylum by a doctor:

> *He is suffering from a very bad leg and cannot earn a living at present. He has been referred on admission at the Adelaide Hospital for want of room. He is quite without means.*

*

Martha would soon be comforted in her grief by the kindly Otto Juncken, who would visit her regularly in Richmond to offer support and friendship. He would have a strong impact upon her life, and her upon his. Otto's background was Danish (on his father's side) and Irish (on his mother's side – Fitzgerald). Otto's father, also Otto, hailed from a German-speaking part of Denmark before moving to Australia and settling in the Barossa Valley, where a large group of Prussians had established themselves. He had a large family in Australia with his wife Margaret as Otto junior had five brothers (Herman, Louis, Charles, Franz Thomas and Albert) and three sisters (Augusta Amalia, Emma Louisa and Anna Ellen).

It was likely that the Needles knew the Juncken brothers from Port Adelaide, as Otto and his brother Charles were carpenters (like Henry Needle) who had been working with Mr Henry Burge's building business, Burge and Kestel, which had built many prominent buildings around Port Adelaide. Burge was a successful builder, councilor and prominent member of the community who left several legacies to charitable organisations and services. Half of Otto's family were working in the Port which at that time was a hive of activity. Brother Louis was a saddler and harness maker who had trained at Holden and Frost saddlery, Grenfell Street, Adelaide and then worked for Mr Brady's saddlery at the Port. Their sister Emma was married to Mr John Samuel Jones junior of *Port Adelaide News and Le Fevre's Peninsula Advertiser*, which would be a useful vehicle for Otto to express himself regarding his later troubles with Martha.

The Junckens had previously worked for their father in Lyndoch in the Barossa Valley before times became economically tough during the 1890s depression, when Otto moved to Victoria with his brother Louis looking for work. Industrious Louis set up his own saddlery and harness store in Richmond, Melbourne. The Juncken brothers first stayed at the Nicholson boarding house where Henry and Martha were reacquainted with them, and Martha later had invited them over to her house for birthday parties. Even though they were devout Christians like Martha, the Juncken family were likely to be Lutherans like the other locals, whose families had settled in the Barossa Valley from Prussia generations earlier because of their strong faith[49] (his mother, an Irish Fitzgerald, would have likely converted to Lutheranism). In July 1890, nine months after her husband died, Martha was back in Melbourne. She continued to keep boarders at Cubitt Street, Richmond. In August, Martha was walking along Swanston Street, the spine of the city of Melbourne, lined with St Paul's Cathedral, the State Library, the Queen Victoria Buildings, and the Town Hall, with the Shot Tower high in the distance. She suddenly spotted the handsome Otto Juncken with his wavy dark hair, large open eyes, tall posture and smart dress.

---

49    Because of their strict Lutheran beliefs and persecution following their resistance to change the practice of Lutheranism by the then ruler of Prussia.

He was just a bit younger than Martha. Before she bumped into Otto on the street, she had not seen either of the Juncken brothers in a very long time.

'Why, hello Mr Otto Juncken,' she said. 'Have you forgotten me?'

'Oh, hello Martha!' said Otto. 'I was very sorry to hear about your loss.'

'I think it very unkind that none of your family has come to see me in my trouble,' Martha said. Devoutly religious and kind-hearted Otto promised Martha that he would soon come and visit her, and quickly arranged a suitable time.

Otto soon started visiting Martha, Elsie and May in August 1890 and the children were excited to have a visitor. Otto brought along bread and flowers. From then on, Otto started to visit about every three weeks and Otto was a godsend when Martha needed it. The children loved the kindly Otto, as did Martha. He was nothing like her husband Henry; he was gentle, caring, hardworking and successful.

However, only two months after these visits commenced, in October 1890, Elsie took sick. She had just turned six years old and was starting to lose her baby teeth. She was wasting away from starvation, and her face was swelling. It was very hard for Martha to make ends meet, as she had only the money from the widow's insurance fund and occasional boarders due to the harsh economic times. Martha was struggling to find paying boarders.

From 1890 to 1893, Australia was in the midst of a severe economic depression (more severe and extended than the 1930s depression[50]) and many banks and building societies collapsed

---

50   Frost, A. (undated). Kew Historical Society. Kew in the 1890s depression.
     http://kewhistoricalsociety.org.au/khs/wp-content/uploads/Kew-in-the-1890s-
     Depression-1.pdf

or suspended payments. Established banks closed as a result, including the large Federal Bank of Australia and the Commercial Bank of Australia (which had built the impressive building on Collins Street, Melbourne). Thousands of people became unemployed and rallied in the streets to highlight their plight. Non-union labour was employed by the Pastoralists' Union of graziers and farmers, and the Maritime Union responded by refusing to load wool, with other unions engaging in strike action. Adelaide was the first place to experience the depression and engage in this strike action which then dispersed across the nation, quickly to be broken up by the Colonial governments, with the aid of police and soldiers.[51] Labor politicians such as stonemason Tom Price (later premier of South Australia) were coming to the fore and battling for better working conditions (especially for women and girls in factories)[52] and the health and safety of workers, and women's suffrage was being vigorously debated.

In 1891, Martha was also one of 30,000 women who had signed the women's suffrage 'Monster petition' put forward to the Parliament of Victoria. In 1894, a similar great petition with 11,600 signatures was collected in South Australia on separate paper sheets pasted together, leading it to be the first colony in Australia to grant women's suffrage in 1894 (thanks to the likes of Mary Lee, Catherine Helen Spence and supporters such as Edward Stirling). Women's suffrage was a way off in Victoria, which did not grant women the right to vote until Federation in 1901.

Otto's visits to Martha became more frequent the sicker Martha's daughter Elsie became. Otto observed of Martha

51   Australia in the 1890s: http://www.myplace.edu.au/decades_timeline/1890/ decade_landing_11.html?tabRank=2&subTabRank=1
52   McCarthy, S. (2015). Tom Price: from Stone cutter to Premier. Wakefield Press. South Australia

that during Elsie's illness, 'no one could have been more tender.' Elise died just a few months after her illness commenced, on 9th December 1890. She was buried at the Kew Cemetery two days later in the same grave as her father. Dr Hodgson declared that she had died from 'gangrenous stomatitis and exhaustion.' Gangrenous stomatitis is a condition related to poor socioeconomic circumstances which was predominantly found in severely malnourished children living in poor hygiene, and often commences when children lose their baby teeth. It begins with a mouth ulcer, face swelling and excessive salivation, and leads to the destruction of oral tissue and bone, and ultimately facial disfigurement. At the time, it appeared to the doctor that the cause of Elsie's death was clear-cut and related to poverty and malnourishment.

Six months later, in 1891, Martha again paid a visit to her family in Adelaide with her daughter May. She visited her sister Ellen Lee who resided at Marrabel, near Hamilton, north of Kapunda. By this time Ellen had six children, the youngest of whom was three-year-old Alexander (Alick) Lee; Ellen would go on to have another six children. When Martha arrived in South Australia to visit her sister, she caught the wrong train and ended up at Farrell's Flat instead of Saddleworth, on route to Hamilton. The stationmaster Mr Clayer, seeing that she had caught the wrong train, invited her into his private home to have afternoon tea with him and his wife.

*Whilst there she spoke freely of her past married life, she then being a widow. She alluded to her unhappiness while in that state owing to the jealousy and cruel acts of her late husband, and avowed her intention of being careful before committing herself again. Mrs Needle is described by Mrs Clayer, the station master's wife, as being thin, a good-looking, cheerful young woman with short curly hair, and she was accompanied by a pretty little curly-headed girl, her daughter.*[53]

Back in Richmond, in July 1891, the 'pretty little curly headed' May also became sick. May was declared by the local doctor to be suffering from marasmus,[54] a form of malnutrition where there is protein energy deficiency, resulting in muscle wasting and characterised by very loose, hanging skin, diarrhoea and dehydration. The real cause of this disease is extreme poverty, and in developing countries, up to two million children still die from this disease. From the time May became ill, Otto Juncken started visiting on a daily basis. He later said that *'when the child was ill, my sympathies were aroused, and my visits were frequent.'*[55] Eventually, May died, on 27th August 1891, officially from tubercular meningitis.[56] The symptoms of meningitis include vomiting, fever, diarrhoea, loss of appetite and irritability. May was buried two days after her death in the Kew Cemetery, in the same grave as her father and sister.

With her husband and two children now dead, Martha was living in desperate times. Despite its impressive skyline with Temperance coffee houses, Melbourne had many inner-city slums, with children playing in laneways with open drains. At this time Martha was still living at 134 Cubitt Street, Richmond. Numbers 128, 129, 130, 131 and 132 Cubitt Street were all vacant – there were many empty houses during the depression

---

53    The Advertiser 16th June 1894
54    The Argus, 27th September 1894.
55    Transcript of trial of Martha Needle
56    The Age, The Richmond Poison Case, 27th September 1894.

years in Melbourne as people were offloading property that was losing value, and they were becoming insolvent and/or leaving the region to look for new opportunities.[57]

*

In October 1891, Martha was clearly mentally and emotionally unwell, and went back to Adelaide to recuperate for some months, on the suggestion of Louis Juncken, who had offered Martha to be his housekeeper in Richmond, though he realised that whilst her child May was ill she could not make the decision to undertake such a task. Otto Juncken had great empathy for Martha as she was quite without means. He was the one who had suggested to his brother Louis that she would make a good housekeeper as she had kept boarders for years. Otto saw first-hand how tenderly she had cared for Elsie and May when they were sick. However, he was entirely oblivious to the hand that Martha had played in their deaths.

During her time in Adelaide, Martha initially stayed with her mother at Hilton, before moving in with a friend at Birkenhead, Port Adelaide (this may have been Henry Needle's family, who lived at Birkenhead). Mary had taken Martha and her brother John to court for not supporting her financially. During this period, it was 'obligatory upon children able to do so to contribute to the old age pension of a parent,' and entry into the Destitute Asylum depended upon an assessment of the alternative family support available. The case against Martha and her brother John was dismissed at the Police Courts due to the lack of means of both children.[58]

---

57   Kew in the 1890s, op cit.
58   The Advertiser, 7th January 1892

Martha often had the appearance of a wealthy woman, although she was far from it. A photographic studio shot taken in 1892 by a photographer in Bridge Road, Richmond, shows Martha finely dressed. In the photograph, which may have been taken shortly after the death of her children, she is wearing a long dark velvety dress which emphasises her busty and curvaceous figure. Her jacket has puffed sleeves, a high choker collar fit with a shiny brooch, silk edging at the bottom and bright metallic buttons at the bottom of the arms and middle of the jacket. Pinned to the top of her jacket is a bouquet with many flowers including lilies and pieces of fern. On her left hand, she has a heavy bracelet and a glove. Her right hand is gloveless and resting on the end spike of an open gate, which is attached to an old large bricked wall. She looks surer of herself than in the earlier photograph, with an extremely stoic look as she stares straight out into the distance, facing what awaits her.

*

With few alternative opportunities, Martha had finally decided to move back to Melbourne and take up the offer of Louis Juncken to be his housekeeper. So in 1892, Martha was offered some reprieve from her difficulties when she took up as a tenant in the living quarters of the house on 137 Bridge Road, Richmond, and to keep boarders. Louis, Otto and Charles worked very hard and their businesses came to prosper. Two weeks after her arrival back to Melbourne in January 1892, Martha and two other boarders, the Winwood brothers from the Cubbitt Street house, moved in with the Junckens. She rented the back part of the Juncken saddler's shop. One of the Winwood brothers soon left, and Charles Juncken and Stanley

Sethwood moved in. Martha finally had some financial security but was prone to moods and strange behaviour.

The Juncken brothers went away to Healesville, Victoria in Easter 1892 which had become a tourist destination for Melbournians after it was connected to the railway in 1889. Martha was left in the house at Richmond with boarder Frank Winwood, an electrician. When the Junckens left for their trip, Martha was in a depressive state which had become habitual since she first arrived at the Juncken house. That weekend, Martha had been grieving constantly for her children and took to her bed. She was feeling the absence of her kind friend Otto Juncken who, it appeared, had been supporting her financially. When the Juncken brothers returned, Martha was to be found in an even more troubled state. She was suicidal and expressed the intention of doing away with herself that weekend via a letter, described below.[59] Otto consulted Dr MacColl about Martha, who prescribed an engagement for marriage, and Otto then consulted his older brother Louis, who deemed that Martha was 'a good and virtuous woman' and agreed to the match. Otto was quickly engaged to Martha just two days after his return from Healesville. The letter that Martha had written in desperation was the following:

*Richmond, Friday night, 15<sup>th</sup> April '92*[60]

*My dear friend,*

*You will be shocked I know when you get this note but you must not think that I have been ungrateful for your*

59  'The Richmond Poisoning Case. Mrs Needle Before the City Court. Said to be Subject to Fits.' *The Argus*, Friday 13 July 1894, p 5
60  'The Poisoning Case. Mrs Needle at the City Court.' *The Age*, Friday 13 July 1894, p 6

*kindness. I know that you have [all] tried to make me forget my troubles but I cannot forget for instead of forgetting I feel my loss more every day if only one of my dear little ones had been spared I would not feel life so hard but as it is I have nothing [all my life] I have knowed nothing but trouble. I have tried hard to fight against fate, but I now give it up. Dear Otto you must not think that I am doing this without thought for I have been thinking of it for a long time. Dear Otto it is sweet to know that you have been my friend for I had so few friends and I hope dear that you will forgive me and not think too unkindly of me for I am so tired of a life of suffering and sorrow which has ever been my fate. I am going away but should my body be found I would like to be buried with my dear children. Dear Otto there's more than enough money in the bank to pay you what I owe you, also Mr King and will you kindly send seven pounds to Mrs Gillaty in Birkenhead that I owe her – to you I give the photos of Elsie and May that are framed and hanging over the mantelpiece in my room and will you please take care of Maysies bird while it lives, as you know I would like my sisters to have what I leave in the house, not that it matters very much what becomes of them, only I would not like the Needles to have anything, they have never tried to make my life any happier for me but I am glad to think it will soon be ended and I will be free from so much sorrow and pain, you can never know the sad heart that I have had ever since all my dear little ones have been so cruelly taken from me for ever, with kind regards to all my boys, and to you dear Otto a fond and last good-bye from*

*Your unhappy friend,*
*Martha Needle*

Martha did not completely recover, despite the 'prescribed engagement' and another housekeeper Mrs Georgina Lillis, a machinist from Burnley, was called in to the Bridge Road household to take care of the housework and attend the boarders. Martha and Georgina became good friends.

Around November 1892, Martha was again summoned to the police court in Adelaide for failure to support her mother. She returned to Melbourne a month later. Not long after her return, trouble set in the Richmond house. Older brother Louis was suddenly not so agreeable to the match between his younger brother Otto and Martha. Martha's depressive episodes were combined with fierce outbursts of temper. From May to August 1893, Martha started complaining to Otto about Louis's cold manner toward her, which continued for over a year. In defiance, in May 1883, Otto wrote to his mother affirming his decision to marry Martha.

By November 1893, Louis was worried enough about the potential match between Otto and the tempestuous Martha that he wrote to his mother in Lyndoch with his concerns and expressed disapproval of the match. Otto's father, who had taken an oath to be a Constable for the Lyndoch Valley, had died in 1890, and as the eldest son Louis assumed responsibility for his younger brother. In response to the letter from Louis, his mother Margaret Juncken (nee Fitzgerald) wrote back to Otto to advise him not to marry Martha, due to her ongoing ill health.

Otto reported the contents of this letter to Martha, whereupon Martha fired off an angry letter to Mrs Juncken who responded by writing to her son urging him not to marry Martha, due to her ill-temperedness and poor health. Martha was so upset about Mrs Juncken's interference in the match that when she visited her friend Eliza Martin, she told her she wanted to kill her. For Martha, Mrs Juncken was an evil and obstructive force, whilst to Margaret Juncken, Martha was a deeply troubled and dangerous individual with an uncontrollable temper.

Martha's awareness of Louis's opposition to her match with Otto further strained their relationship. It was only resolved when Louis became suddenly ill, and Martha started to care for him. A familiar pattern had emerged. Louis first became ill in April 1893, when Martha attended to him and he recovered. In August 1893, Louis again took sick and Martha was again attentive toward him, and continued to nurse him until a professional nurse was called in. However, 30 year old Louis eventually died May 16th 1894, at the Bridge Road house. The Juncken family reported the news of Louis's death back in Adelaide, in *The Register*.

When Dr S. MacColl issued the death certificate, he declared the cause of death to be 'Gastritis and Endocarditis.' However, Dr Grant suggested that Louis might have died due to poisonous matter in his stomach. Dr MacColl said he wished to examine the heart of Louis in the name of medical science, for he had never seen a case like it. Otto said that he did not wish to take the responsibility for this, and that he would ask his deeply religious mother for consent. Dr MacColl remarked that 'It does not matter bothering, as you do not consent.' The newspapers later reported that Dr MacColl had wished an autopsy to be undertaken but the family did not wish this to occur.

Shortly after his brother's death, Herman arrived in Melbourne from the Barossa Valley, along with his mother, to take care of the transport of Louis's body back to the Colony of South Australia for the burial and funeral service. Relations between Martha and Mrs Juncken were initially cold, with self-centred Martha accusing the grief-stricken Mrs Juncken of not speaking to her. Otto went with his mother and brother back to Lyndoch to attend his brother's funeral, before returning to Richmond with Herman and his sister Mrs Emma Jones, who were to help organise his brother's business affairs.

Herman stayed at the Bridge Road house whilst his sister Emma stayed with friends, the Smiths, in Sherwood Street, around the corner. One day, Herman went to pay a visit to the nearby Smith's house and took ill (having just eaten with Martha at Bridge Road). Little Alice Smith came to tell Otto that Herman was sick and was going to stay there. When Otto visited the Smith's house, Herman vomited in front of him. Otto, concerned that the condition from which Louis died from was contagious, immediately contacted Dr Boyd and arranged for him to pay a house visit. He reported to the doctor that his brother Louis had died of gastritis to which the doctor replied 'That is a strange cause of death.' Dr Boyd immediately suspected poisoning, and asked for the vomit of Herman to be preserved for testing. Herman had begun to notice that his sickness occurred after he had eaten food or beverages served by Martha, and he made a visit to the police.

As the police were suspicious of poisoning, they planned a trap to determine if poisoning was playing a role in Herman's sickness. They planned for Herman to visit Martha and ask for a cup of tea, whilst Detectives Whitney and Fryer waited out the front of the house at Richmond. Herman went back to the saddlery at Richmond and asked for a cup of tea. At one stage Martha asked him to go and fetch some milk from next door. After he came back into the kitchen, she poured the milk into the tea and served it to her fiancé's brother.

Herman tasted the tea and noticed a bitter taste, before putting back onto the table. 'It tastes bitter'.

'Why, it's just tea.'

Herman made an excuse to go outside and gave the waiting detectives a signal for the police to enter the house. They shortly arrived inside the house to confiscate the cup of tea served by Martha to Herman, along with her own tea, and have it examined for arsenic poisoning. Martha was shocked to see them. Martha turned towards Herman and asked, 'Have you done this Herman?'

Herman could only reply, 'Yes.'

After seizing the cups of tea, the detectives scoured the house for evidence of poison and other circumstantial evidence that might suggest a motive for the attempted poisoning and the suspected poisoning of Louis.

Detective Whitney asked Martha 'Do you have any poison in the house?'

Martha was surprised but quite indignant, 'No, there is no poison in this house. At least, I do not think so.'

Whitney and Fryer then made their way around the house, going upstairs where the bedrooms were and examining every room for bottles of poison, followed by Herman and Martha. When they went to enter Martha's bedroom, she went ahead of them and attempted to seize a bottle of chlorodyne, but was prevented from doing so by Whitney.[61]

'Do you want to poison yourself?' asked Whitney.

'I would be much more likely to do that than to poison anyone else,' said Martha.

The detectives then found other bottles containing liniment, iodine and chlorodyne which they confiscated. Going back downstairs, the Detectives scoured the kitchen cupboards and finally found a box of 'Rough on Rats.'

---

61  'A Sensational Poisoning Story. Alleged Attempted Murder. Arrest of a Widow.' *The Argus*, Thursday 14 June 1894 p 5

'Where did you get this box?' asked Whitney.

'At the shop of Mr Richards, the chemist on Swan Street at Richmond,' replied Martha.

The detectives seized the box and bottles and carefully took away the two cups of tea for examination. They arrested Martha for the suspected poisoning of Louis and took her away from the property to lock her up in the City Watch House, whilst she waited trial at the Melbourne City Police Court.

# 5

# A Sensational Poisoning Story

The story of Martha Needle's arrest for attempting to poison Herman Juncken first broke in the Melbourne newspapers on 14^th June, 1894. Stories of her arrest and trial were a popular feature of the late 19^th century tabloids across Australia and New Zealand. *The Argus* also alluded to a further investigation into Martha's crimes, sensationally suggesting that Martha was responsible for the death of Louis Juncken, Herman's brother, her husband and children, charges that had not yet been laid. These reports were all made *prior to* the news relayed on 18th June that the detectives in the case were going to approach the South Australian authorities to arrange an exhumation of Louis Juncken who was buried at Lyndoch in the Barossa Valley. Even the *New York Times* reported on the range of these alleged crimes on 16^th June, 1894, before any further charges had been laid:

### Alleged Woman
### Poisoner

*Melbourne, June 15^th-Mrs Martha Needle, widow, keeper of a lodging house, has been arrested on the charge of attempting to kill one of her lodgers, a man named Juncken, by*

*giving him arsenic. The authorities have begun an inves-*
*tigation of the case, and from discoveries made believe that*
*the woman's husband and three children and Juncken's*
*brother, all of whom died recently, were poisoned by her.*[62]

Martha quickly became known as 'The Black Widow' and 'The Poisoner' of the *'Richmond Poisoning Case'*. The case was tried in the press well before the Police Court and Supreme Court cases, with some evidence including letters written by Martha and Otto being made freely available to the press by the police investigating the case.[63] The case was all the more sensational as Martha was a well-presented and good-looking young woman who challenged traditional notions of what it was to be a good wife and mother yet, from all outward appearances, portrayed this exactly. This was at a time when motherhood was seen as 'natural' and instinctual for women and public roles for women were limited.

Throughout the newspaper reports were attempts to under-stand the tragic events and motivations for Martha's alleged crimes. Extraordinarily, some newspapers claimed that Martha came from a well-known and respectable family and was a well-presented, 'well to do' woman. This may have been due to her care for her appearance. Mr Wilkes, a Farrier of Currie Street, Adelaide, had rented out a house to Mary Foran at Hilton during her stay in Adelaide in 1892, and recollected Martha's visit. Even though Martha was quite poor, Wilkes had the impression that Martha was prosperous due to being well dressed.[64] There was also suggestion that there was freehold

---

62   The New York Times, 16th June 1894

63   The Richmond Poisoning Case. The Letters of the Accused. A Vow to Kill Mrs. Juncken. Life Assurances Affected. The Argus, Saturday 16 June 1894 p 7 Article

64   The Advertiser, 16th June 1894

property owned by Martha's family in South Australia, which was far from the real situation of her mother and step father regularly frequenting the Destitute Asylum.[65]

Other newspapers claimed that she was driven by poverty and the insurance money, a violent husband and her passion for Otto. Dire poverty may have led her to try to quickly obtain the insurance money, she did have a violent husband and a passion for Otto (with whom she became reacquainted after the death of her husband), but none of these really fully explained her motives if she was guilty.

A picture was also painted of Martha of a charming, flirtatious character who easily attracted the attention of a large number of suitors, arousing the jealousy of her watchful husband.[66] It was said that 'Mrs Needle was of a flighty disposition, fond of company, with a weakness for the admiration of the sterner sex, which was invariably accorded to her. Her husband was of a very jealous disposition, and the inevitable discord and daily jarring in the domestic circle was the result. Needle, it appears, was of a retiring disposition, and little was ever seen of him by visitors to the house.'[67]

Otto was presented as a devoutly religious and caring man, dedicated to making the poor woman happy in an idyllic future, after a miserable start in life and violent first husband.[68] However, Martha and Otto never had an idyllic start, as they became engaged after she had threatened suicide. In addition, once her relationship with Otto was threatened by Louis and Mrs Juncken, Martha wavered between being vengeful and threatening to kill Mrs Juncken, and threatening her own life.

---

65   The Pictorial Australian May June 1894
66   The Register 16th June 1894
67   Evening Standard, 14th July 1894
68   The Argus, 16th June 1894

According to the highly sensationalist *The Pictorial Australian* report, Otto tried to destroy the following letter when the detectives searched the household. Many letters such as this one were supposedly marked 'to be destroyed':

'To Otto –

*I have once set my heart on something which only fair consent and acquiescence will secure to me and which I have settled for many a year. I shall enjoy it more if you bestow it graciously. You will remember I have repeatedly expressed this wish.*

*I once thought I won your unalienated heart. Pride sternly sets food upon this spark of hope with cruel insistence. Your love has never been mine, and defrauded of the diamond can I accept and patiently wear the paste. Dear, I propose at least a temporary change in our relations...*

*When you asked me to become your wife neither of us contemplated this cruel separation your unkind and heartless mother has involved upon us, and for your sake, not hers, I am unwilling to fetter you by an engagement, and want you to be entirely free, bound by no promises; your heart shall no longer be burdened by bonds which I can loosen, because your peace and happiness are more to me than my own. I grant you complete release for twelve months. If after than you consider me necessary to you, then you can have a renewal of your bonds.*

*Martha*

*P.S. Dear Otto, I feel very ill, and I sincerely hope this will be my last illness, as I am so tired of life, as you know I have no happiness to look back upon and none to look forward to. If it was not for the fear that I would not meet my dear little ones and yours in the spirit land I would pass away this night, and you please remember if I am tempted to do away with my miserable life, on your hands and your wicked mother's rests the sin. If I get worse please don't bring a doctor, for I will not see him.*

*Martha'*[69]

When Martha Needle was arrested, two women came forth to the local media in Adelaide claiming to be Mrs Needle's mother. A woman from Birkenhead initially made the claim (possibly Mrs Hannah Needle, her mother-in-law, who lived in Birkenhead) as well as her actual mother, Mary Foran. As she was illiterate, Mary would have relied upon information being passed on to her about her daughter Martha being arrested in the Colony of Victoria (as indicated by the X mark on her marriage certificate). Mary would also pass on stories to fuel the newspapers and was particularly vocal in her opinion of Martha's capacity to commit the crimes she was accused of. She told *The SA Register* that Martha had left home when she was twelve years old and had threatened to poison her.[70]

Upon Martha's arrest, Otto organised and paid for one of the most experienced and prominent lawyers in the Colony of Victoria to defend his fiancé, 48 year old David Gaunson, an already well-established solicitor when he represented the famous bushranger Ned Kelly in his pre-trials fourteen years earlier. Not only a lawyer, Gaunson was also a politician, a young Liberal who later became a Labor candidate. He was described as a good-looking and convivial person who 'enjoyed

---

69   The Argus, 16th June 1894
70   The Register, 16th June 1894

the spotlight,'[71] and was a favourite at social gatherings, but who in court had a sharp and unforgiving wit.[72] He had a temper and was sometimes considered an 'unruly' member of parliament. Gaunson's sense of humour and outbursts of temper are evident in the transcripts and newspaper reports of the police and Supreme Court trials of Martha Needle. Raised religious and having learnt to play the church organ, he 'abandoned churchgoing and stated that he worshipped God according to his conscience.'[73] He had 'boasted that he had cheated Pentridge prison of more deserving tenants than any other practitioner in Victoria.'[74] He was 'legal counsel to Madame Brussels, of Melbourne's most famous brothel, and the Licensed Victualler's Association' and also 'had links with the railwaymen's trade union.'[75]

Gaunson had a firm belief in justice for all. During this period in the colony, the accused were not able to give evidence at their trial, and Gaunson often used the media, in particular *The Age* newspaper, to get interviews with key people published to present his clients' side of the case. This tactic would prove difficult in the Martha Needle case when all of the newspapers leaked evidence and appeared to immediately assume her guilt.

On Saturday, 16th June 1894, Gaunson made an application for bail in the City Police Court to Mr Keogh, Police Magistrate, and other members of the all-male bench (Messrs Charles Cooke, S. Lancashire, Thomas Learmonth, H Cherry and Bowley, Justices of the Peace).

---

71  The Crown v Edward Kelly, David Gaunson, flier. Old Melbourne Gaol.
72  Obituaries Australia, David Gaunson (1846-1909) and Australian Dictionary of Biography, David Gaunson by Geoffrey Serle, Australian National University.
73  ibid
74  ibid
75  ibid

Gaunson supported his application with what *The Weekly Times* journalist described as 'an interesting speech.' Gaunson took on the press reports on the case when he applied for bail on behalf of Mrs Needle. One thing going against Martha being released on bail was the concern that she would die by suicide. Approaching the Police Court bench, Gaunson acknowledged the seriousness of the case, but said that the difficulties experienced in the defence of Martha were exacerbated by the extent to which the daily newspapers were publishing on the case. He said that he was concerned that Martha would not receive a fair trial as a result of these press reports. He also claimed to the bench that it was difficult to work up his defence with Martha being in jail. He claimed that she was in a 'low state of health' and was not getting the proper attention or food in jail that she required. Others on remand were allowed to get food from outside the prison, but this was not a privilege Martha had been afforded. Gaunson was forceful and antagonistic in his speech to the bench which, predictably, was widely reported on in the newspapers.

Gaunson said, 'It must be, not that the woman has poison on herself which could be discovered by searching her clothes, but that some person would poison her if her food were sent in from outside. What a grotesque reason is that? For this reason, this unfortunate woman, who is in a low and miserable state of health, is compelled to put up with whatever the gaol compels her to accept as food. Of course, it is supposed she might be murdered by the food sent in it may as well be to remember that she might be killed in another way, for there is such a thing as judicial murder. We all know that. I am not in any way complaining of the discretion which is being exercised, but the accused would be in a position to give proper instructions, and to do this she should have the common necessaries – I can't say comforts – to enable her health to be such that she can come to meet the accusation.'

'I don't know whether the newspapers are engaged in an attempt or a conspiracy to hang this woman, but it looks something like it. The statements which have been published are likely to prevent her from obtaining fair trial, and the whole community is being poisoned against her. I can't blame the newspapers for giving an extraordinary case every detail, but still there is a dividing line in the mind of every reasonable person, and that line they have overstepped in this case.'

Joseph Brown was a police officer and Superintendent of Detectives in the Criminal Investigation Branch working on the case, and some press articles had reported that they had received their stories from Brown. Gaunson rightly said that Brown had not explicitly publicly stated the charges against Martha, although there were numerous insinuations in the press.

'You have read that this important person is not before you merely on the charge before you, but also on charges not yet levelled against her – on charges of murdering her husband and of having murdered her three children, and of having murdered Louis Juncken. Of course, Mr Brown is too astute an officer to mention these as charges against her. He probably will say that she has attempted her own life – that she administered poison to herself, that on occasion, perhaps, fortunately for her, a doctor was called in, and was the means of her recovery. The only point your Worship will have to consider will be that, but I have never heard yet of it being a ground for refusing bail that there is a prospect of the accused poisoning herself.'

The media became part of a jury that had not yet sat, and Martha's 'happy demeanour'[76] was noted by reporters and declared 'unwomanly.'

*When in durance, women, as a rule, give way to futile repining, but Mrs Needle is the rare exception. Outwardly nothing seems to cause her real concern, whatever may be her feelings.*

*The Register 21st June 1894*

Gaunson appealed to the Police Court Jurors regarding the conduct of the media. 'She is not a convicted person but only an accused person. I therefore ask you in dealing with this matter to say the only consideration is will it be likely that she will appear when called on for trial. I can take it for granted you will not listen to the rubbish printed in the newspapers. It is the proprietors who are to blame for that and their conduct may be investigated in another court. I conclude by asking that the bail be reasonable and not prohibitory.'

When Gaunson had finished his appeal, Superintendent Brown, spoke to the bench, alluding to Martha Needle as being at risk of suicide. 'I would ask your Worship to hear a little evidence to show that the accused is likely, if liberated on bail, to do what she has attempted to do before, and what she attempted to do when arrested.'

Gaunson interjected on Brown's claims, 'The Superintendent's remarks are unfair.'

Superintendent Brown asserted, 'If she were liberated she would not appear – she would poison herself.'

It was Detective-Sergeant Whitney's turn to speak. 'At the arrest of Mrs Needle, she attempted to secure a bottle of chlorodyne which was in her room. From enquiries I made, I found Mrs Needle had on several occasions tried to commit suicide by taking poison. Another poison, 'Rough on Rats,' was in her possession.'

---

76   The Argus, 19th June 1894

It is not actually clear if Martha had ever made an attempt on her own life, or just threatened to do so. It is unlikely that she would have done so, as it appears at that time that she was optimistic that she would be released from prison. Martha did not realise the reality or seriousness of her predicament, as indicated in letters from Otto to Martha's friend Mrs Owen, where he refers to her as 'poor Martha' and 'poor girl' as 'she thinks everything will be okay.'[77]

Grasping at straws, Gaunson suggested that Herman may have poisoned his own tea with intent in order to set Martha up. He asked Detective-Sergeant Whitney, 'Did you search Herman Juncken before you went to Mrs Needle's house?'

'No' replied the Detective-Sergeant.

'But you knew he was against her marrying his brother?' asked Gaunson.

'I did not at the time.'

'Can you suggest anyone likely to poison her?' asked Gaunson.

'No, I do not know of anyone.'

'Do you know of any reason why she should not be allowed to receive ordinary food from friends outside?'

'No, it is the orders of the Governor of the gaol.'

Gaunson ceased his questioning, Whitney retired from the witness box, and it was finally left to the bench to decide on the application for bail.

After the bench returned from discussion, Mr Keogh, Police Magistrate, spoke. 'The bench are of the opinion that the accused should not be allowed out under bail under the circumstances mentioned.'[21] Martha would be living in a cell for the foreseeable future.

---

77   Letters from Otto to Ada Owen 2/8/94.

Despite Gaunson's attempt to minimise the press reporting on the case, the newspapers across Australia continued stories about Martha and interviewed associates of Martha. Many of the stories appear to be fabrication, whilst others were informed by the extraordinary leaking to the press of evidence in the form of letters and other private documents of Martha and Otto held by the police.[78] A dark portrait was painted of Martha Needle's character. *The Argus* stated that when Martha left home 'her relationships with her parents were strained, and subsequently she was violent towards her mother, who feared her exceedingly.'[79] It was even claimed that Mrs Foran was hospitalised due to her 12 year old daughter's violence toward her, far from the real situation where Daniel Foran sexually abused the 12 year old Martha and then beat up his wife Mary.

*The Argus* claimed that the animosity that existed between Martha and her mother was linked to Martha's belief – more likely a symptom of dissociation – that her mother was not her real mother after all. Martha believed that her 'faux mother' Mary was preventing her from receiving a £700 legacy left by her father when he died, who was allegedly heir to a property in Chancery. The story alleged that Martha's birth father had supposedly returned to England after he left his wife, and then came back to Australia, only to die around 1873. The missed legacy allegedly created conflict between mother and daughter. Letters published in the papers claimed that Martha was trying to find out her 'true identity'[80] and if she had any brothers and sisters, when in fact it was clear that she knew whom her older sisters were throughout her

---

78   The Register 19th June 1894
79   The Argus, 18th June 1894
80   The Argus, 20th June 1894

life, and it was likely that she was suffering a delusion about a rich father and her faux mother. Interestingly, the meaning of 'in Chancery' is being in a 'hopeless predicament'[81] which is the situation Martha was in.

The newspapers in Melbourne claimed that Martha had hired a detective to seek the true identity of her parents. Many of Martha's letters, with incorrect spelling, appeared in their pages. One of these letters (complete with spelling errors) found and published was written under alias Mr Delbroke, which supposedly revealed Martha's attempt to discover clues about her early life, and her mother's very real cruelty (supported by contemporary accounts). There was no 'Mr Delbroke' living in Melbourne at this time.[82] The letter included below is in its original spelling.

Melbourne, Dec 4. 1893

*To Mr Foran,*

*Sir, - It will be gratley to your advantge if you will kindly send to me all pertuclers[83] and informashion concerning that little girl you had living with you and your wife when you lived in Port Lincoln and North Adelaide. She was known as Martha Charles when she grew up, and I want you to tell me whos Child she was, for I know that you know all about her. Was she Mrs.Forans own child. If not, who is her mother and father, and wher did you wif get her frome, for we do not think that any mother could be as crewl to her one child as she was to that little girl. Please*

---

81  Merriam-Webster Dictionary: https://www.merriam-webster.com/dictionary/chancery
82  According to Sands and MacDougall Directories
83  particulars

*tell me if you now wher Martha Charles is now, and if she has got any brothers ore sisters, and wher was she born, and how old she is. It will be to your agvantge to give all the informiton that you know concraing[84] that child.*

*Yours, A.F.*
*Delbroke, G.P.O.,*
*Melbourne.*

*The Argus, 19th June 1894*

The newspapers also claimed that in another letter, Martha wrote to a former colleague of Mr Foran's, Mr Bartlett, who was in fact the warden at St Thomas Church, Port Lincoln, where Martha had grown up. The spelling in this letter is poor, which may have reflected Martha's mental health at the time of writing, as she did not even spell her own name correctly or that of its intended recipient, and there were several spellings of the surname 'Kenedy.' In her likely pronunciation it also suggests a slight Scottish accent. The letter is extremely sad as it also shows Martha asked about her real mother and she refused to believe that Mary was her real mother, due to her 'unwomanly treatment' towards her.

137 Bridge Roade, Richmond

*To Mr.Barklet,*
*Sir,*

*I hope you will excuse the liberty, but It is a matter of grat importance to me. I wish to ask you if you can recoll to memery a family that worked for you about 16 or 20 years*

---

84  concerning

*ago cald Foran or better known as Kinddy – they had a little girl with them cauld Marther. Do you remember she was left to look after Foran or Kinddy and 2 little boys when he, Kineday, worked for you cutting hay at a palace[85] called Petoper ore sume such name while Mrs.Kineady was In the Adelaide hospital with a bad leag. Well Sir can you tell me wither that Child Martha was her onne child, as I fell very doubtful about It and Mrs Foran will not tell me where the child was boran nor the name of anyone that kew the girl wile she was very young: so knowing that you know them If you can only recall them to member thy also lived on a station named Lake Hamaltion[86], but I can not rightly remember the name of the oversears or I would write to him. The Kinadys also lived at the Little Swampe, and I think they worked for a gentleman named Allright, but I am not sure about his name. Hoping this will not put you to too much trouble. If you Can give me eny information Concarning that girl Martha you will be doing a kindness to one that has sufferd very much frome Mrs Kinadys unwomanly treatment.*

*Yours sincerely*
*M. Needle.*

*The Argus, 19th June 1894*

The newspapers turned to the discord in the relationship between Martha and Henry and the thwarted relationship between Martha and Otto to explain the motives for Martha's alleged crimes. The following abridged letter was published in newspapers and was written by Martha when Otto was

---

85   place
86   Lake Hamilton

in Lyndoch only one week after Louis's death, and Martha's poor spelling was corrected for publication in the newspaper. This was presented as 'Exhibit A' in the case of Regina versus Martha Needle, in full.

*Richmond, May 22, 1894*

*To Otto*

*You could leave your grief-stricken mother long enough to write to me in this manner. Well, this is as I expected, for I knew your dear mother would make you see things with her eyes as she has done before You try to excuse her by saying she wanted to see me on Friday morning to thank me for my kindness to your brother. Well, that she could have done while she was here if she so wished. One would have thought that as she came over here she could never have rested until she talked to me about her dead child, knowing, as she did, that I was with him through all his illness. She made the excuse to me in the evening that she could not talk and laugh with me. Did you or she think I expected that she could laugh? I did expect that she would speak to me in a friendly way, if only concerning her dead son. She could thank Mrs. Gray for coming out, but to me that had done so much for her children she could not speak. You know that I tried to be friendly with her when she came and before she left, but she would not let me. Surely, Otto, you know in your heart that I did not deserve such treatment. You know that she left this house in the morning without one word to me, and yet you blame me for my cold manner. In the evening after she had been in my house for over four hours, and had never opened her lips to me all that time but she could talk to the old lady about Mr Smith's home very nice talk for a heartbroken mother. I must* say she ought never have left this house until she left with her son's body for Adelaide. I can tell you that your mother's conduct in going from here is the talk of all the <u>road</u>.

You think you dear mother is heart-broken, but she can not pass that off on a woman who has lost all her children. Why, I would never have gone out visiting before your brother was in his grave as his loving mother did while his poor body was lying at the railway station. Why did your wicked mother come over here to make us more unhappy than we were before? If she is the good loving mother that you think she is, why did she not come to see her child before he died, the Doctor over there told her that her son might not get over his illness <u>yet</u> she never came to see him in life and neither should <u>she you</u> if you were doing for she is like the one that is gone, all self. When I asked her if she would like to go up to see her boy after Mrs Gray had gone she said the stairs were too trying for her so she did not forget her own self even at such a time when you told her the poor dog was not Louis's but mine she would not look at it and you say <u>that she</u> entered my house will all ill feelings buried, of course Otto I believe you that she told you so, but could you not see how bitter she was to me when she came and left. Not you can not see any thing wrong that your mother does. <u>You poor fool to say you thought this sad event would cause a reconciliation between her and I.</u> Friday was no day for such talk and even if she wished to make you happy she could have spoken to you alone about that. Between you, you have caused me much misery, and I wonder you are not afraid God would strike you both dead when you are planning my ruin between you.

You would allow your mother to part us if we had been married by all the ministers in the world. For you know

73

*then nothing should have parted us. If you had been an honourable man, or if you wished to make an <u>honourable woman</u> of me – but no, men like you have <u>your turn, and I could be thrown aside</u>. But remember this, the day <u>you</u> cast me off for your mother you will soon be motherless, for I shall kill her if I have to walk every mile from here to Lyndoch. I have vowed to my God to do this, and I shall keep that vow, both you and she shall see what it is to try a woman as I have been – tried by you and yours.*

*Do you think that was right to go and leave me in this death-stricken house so soon and for so long? Would I have left you so long by yourself at a time like this? I would not say one word about you staying so long if your mother had not got her family with her of if you had been the only boy, but as it is I do not know how Otto you could think of leaving me so long by myself.*

*You must not think that I shall not keep my word and kill her if she parts us, for I have quite made up my mind that she shall never cause another woman all the sin and misery she has brought on me. Now you can do whatever you like while you are over at home…I want you to write at once and let me know whether you intend to still board with me, or are you going to do as your mother wishes to do? So let me know at once, as I will only need a very small house for Stanley and myself.*

YOUR CAST-OFF LANDLADY

*P.S. Don't forget to tell your mother confessor all I have done to you.*

*The Weekly Times* ran a full page pictorial spread of all of the main characters in 'The Richmond Poisoning Case' on Saturday, June 23$^{rd}$ 1894, as did *The Australasian*. This included drawings of Martha and Henry (drawn from photos), a picture of Juncken's saddlery shop in Bridge Road, the dead children (with names erroneously ascribed), Dr Boyd, Detectives Fryer and Whitney and a facsimile of one of the hand-written verses of Martha in her own handwriting (complete with spelling errors):

> *Give me back my heart*
> *Give me back my heart again*
> *I'll forget the happy past*
> *You have caused me grief and pain*
> *Shadows over my pathway cast*

> *The Weekly Times 23$^{rd}$ June 1894*

A similar letter appeared in *The Pictorial Australian* ...

> *To A Dear One – Otto*
> *They would give thee to another,*
> *They would break thy vow;*
> *They would give thee to another,*
> *And my heart is lonely now.*
> *They remember not my sorrow,*
> *They remember not my tears;*
> *They would sever in one fatal hour*
> *The tenderness of years. But is*
> *it well to leave me; Wouldst*
> *though so deceive me?*
> *-Martha Needle*

> *The Pictorial Australian May-June 1894*

It is difficult to tell if these verses were the work of Martha or created by journalists to add to the dramatic effect of the story. The tough economic times produced a sense of schadenfreude around the Needle case, and there was immense interest in it. In the absence of television and when pictures were infrequent in the paper, the waxworks were a popular entertainment, and one popular place to view public figures was at Kreitmayer's Melbourne Waxworks Exhibition. The Waxworks were open daily from 9am until 10pm, and the most popular exhibit were the criminals in the 'Chamber of Horrors.'[87] The interest in the Richmond Poisoning Case was such that a waxwork effigy was made of alleged murderess Martha. Mr Gaunson complained of this, and the effigies were taken down from the waxworks display in Melbourne, at the instruction of the Attorney General.[88]

Otto had a very different perspective on Martha, initially believing that she did not commit multiple murders, and then seemingly resigned to thinking that she did commit the murders, but believing that she was not conscious of what she was doing at the time. The ever-faithful Otto, only 29 years of age, rallied Martha's friends around to support her in prison. He frequently wrote to friend Mrs R Owen, Tooronga Road, Upper Hawthorn who would visit with her daughter Ada Owen, a good friend of Martha, to inform her of visiting hours in the prison. Visitors could come together, and Otto would arrange for various friends to meet together or separately to visit Martha on certain days,[89] and these groups always included Mrs Owen. Otto would write to Mrs R Owen, gently encouraging her to visit Martha.

---

87   http://www.glenrowan1880.com/wax.htm

88   The Horsham Times, 10th August 1894

89   Mrs Owen, Mrs Gibbons and Mrs Silverthorne (16th July), Mrs Owen and Mrs
     Martin (26th July) or Mrs Owen, Mrs Gibbons and Mrs Mackney (2nd August).

> 137 Bridge Road
> Richmond
> 16/7/94

Dear Mrs Owen,

Mrs Needle's case has been adjourned until tomorrow week so I daresay you will be able to see her at the Gaol tomorrow if you so wish. As only a visit a day is allowed her and Mrs Gibbons and Mrs Silverthorne are anxious to see her it would be as well if you could meet them at a certain time say 11 o'clock and you could all go in together as that is allowed.

I expected to have seen you up at the court today and I trust that it is not illness that has prevented you from coming. I will try and call out to see you one evening this week when I hope to find both yourself and Ada in good health.

With kind regards
Believe me to be,
Your sincere friend
Otto Juncken

\*

The press eagerly awaited the findings of the chemical analysis to determine if Martha had indeed attempted to poison Herman. The first chemical analysis of the evidence against Martha was made on 20th June by government analyst Mr Cuthbert Blackett[90], which confirmed that

---

90   In 1889 Mr Cuthbert Robert Blackett, government analyst, was listed as a Dentist rather than a Pharmacist, and was also a conservative politician (and member for Fitzroy). Mr Blackett was in fact practicing dentistry with pharmacy before the Act requiring registration for

there was indeed arsenic in the tea Martha had prepared for Herman.

Following this confirmation, the Chief Commissioner of Police sent a request to the Crown Law authorities to make an application to the South Australian government to exhume the body of Louis Juncken, who had now been buried for over a month. On 20th June 1894, Detective Whitney directly served the order for the exhumation of Louis's body to Martha Needle in the Melbourne Gaol, and Martha Needle asked the detective to read the order. Martha was called into court on 21st June again, as Sub-inspector Gardiner asked for a further remand, which was granted. The same day Dr Neild, Detective Whitney and Herman Juncken left for Adelaide and the exhumation of Louis Juncken.

The exhumation of the body of Louis was a big spectacle in the town of Lyndoch, South Australia. A tent was erected in the graveyard and the post-mortem examination was performed on site by Dr Neild who took the liberty of bringing along his son, a medical student. Detective Whitney, Mr H King (undertaker) and Herman Eagle (labourer who dug the grave) also attended. Herman Juncken and his brother-in-law Mr Jones were there to confirm Louis's identity, and Dr Popham from Gawler assisted with the examination. Also present was Constable Hae, Adelaide's 'coroner constable' and Mr Mitchell, the Lyndoch cemetery's curator. The place also swarmed with reporters. One notable absence was Mrs

---

pharmacy was passed. He was not registered as a Pharmacist until 20th March 1888, but was already a member of the Pharmacy Board 11 year prior to this, from 1877. In 1887, Mr Blackett was appointed the acting Government Analyst as the previous Government Analytic Chemist, William Johnson, had died. Shortly after Mr Blackett 'removed his laboratory and office to the College of Pharmacy, Swanston Street, Melbourne – the old County Court.' Mr Blackett was also responsible for analysing imported spirits. In 1888 he was also involved in an evaluation of the conditions in mental asylums.

Margaret Juncken, mother of Louis. The local doctor, Dr Richter, went to the gravesite and asked that she be excused from identifying her son due to her grief and fragile emotional state. Detective Whitney insisted that Mrs Juncken be there, even though Louis's other brothers and brother-in-law were present, and sent a cab for her. Herman came back to the gravesite with his brother-in-law Jones and said that he refused to bring his mother to the site. He was armed with a medical certificate stating that his mother was too unwell to attend, and that she had fainted and been taken away from the funeral. Whitney finally agreed that she should not be brought to the site. After an hour and a quarter of digging, the coffin was reached and raised to ground level. Then suddenly a dramatic scene arose for all the press to see: grief stricken Margaret Juncken arriving with her son Charles to identify her son's body. However, it was Charles and his brother-in-law Jones who finally identified the body of Louis by looking through the glass of the leaden casket.[91]

Astonishingly, the press were allowed to be present at the gravesite examination during this era, and Dr Neild's observations at the post-mortem examination were freely conveyed to them and quickly reported upon in the newspapers the following day.[92] The release of Dr Neild's report incensed Dr S MacColl of Richmond, who had attended to Louis before his death and whose medical judgement was now being publicly questioned. He fired off a letter to the editor of *The Argus*, impatient to defend himself.

*Sir – It has reportedly appeared in the press that endocarditis was the cause certified by me of Louis*

---

91   The Argus, 25 June 1894
92   27th June 1894

*Juncken's death. I now write to say that this was not the case. My certificate was 'Gastritis and Endocarditis,' which is a very different thing.*

*Dr Neild has not been slow to state what he did not find in accordance with my certificate. Ordinary courtesy should have constrained him to state what he did find in accordance with it.*

*The reason for which post-mortem evidence of endocarditis was not found by him will be clear when my evidence is given.*

*Forbearing further comment on this case while sub judice[93] - I am,*

*D. S MacColl M.B. Ch. M.*
*Richmond, June 30<sup>th</sup>*

*The Argus 2<sup>nd</sup> July 1894*

Back in Melbourne, the chemical analysis of Louis's remains was performed by Blackett. His report was quickly made on 26th June, and was released and reported on in the newspapers 29<sup>th</sup> June. The report stated:

*Laboratory, Swanston-Street, June 29, 1894.*

*Interim report to Sergeant Whitney. Criminal Investigation Department in re Regina v Needle – In the stomach and intestines in jar No 1, which I received from you and Detective Fryer on Tuesday morning, I have found that arsenic is present. It also appears to be present in the liver, but I have not had time fully and absolutely to confirm this. Its presence*

---

93   Under judgement

*in jar No 1, sealed by Dr Neild and opened by me, is
unmistakable. C R BLACKETT, Government Analyst.*

*The Pictorial Australian May June 1894*

Blackett's next progress report on the case was similarly
reported on. It should be noted that Martha was not tried for
the attempted murder of Herman Juncken, as reported.

*The Richmond Poisoning Case*

*Further Traces of Arsenic Discovered*

*The analysis will not be complete until Wednesday night.
Meantime, Detective-Sergeant Whitney and Detective Fryer
have finished the briefing of witnesses in the charge of
attempted murder of Herman Juncken proffered against Mrs
Needle. About sixteen witnesses are concerned, and their evidence should not take long. Mrs Needle's health is suffering
under the strain of imprisonment and anxiety, and on Saturday
she was seized with fainting fits, which rendered necessary her
removal to the gaol hospital. Under the care of Dr Shields, the
medical officer, she was somewhat improved yesterday.*

*Blackett's examination as it progresses strengthens the ad
interim report made by him on Friday last, and published
in The Argus on Saturday, in which he stated that in jar
No 1 (part of the stomach and intestines) he had found
unmistakable traces of arsenical poison. There are five jars
altogether, and only one has yet been found to be free of
arsenic. That is the one containing the heart and portion
of the lungs. The others have all, so far as the examination
has gone, yielded traces of poison.*

*The Argus, 2<sup>nd</sup> July 1894*

After Blackett's full report, Detective Whitney charged Martha Needle with wilfully murdering Louis. At that time, she was in the infirmary area of the Old Melbourne Gaol as she had suffered from fainting fits. After the discovery of arsenic in the body of Louis, the Chief Commissioner of Police Mr Chomley took a strong interest in the case, and asked Superintendent Brown to inform him of the circumstances surrounding Henry Needle and his children. Detectives Whitney and Fryer then developed a full report which was sent to Chief Commissioner Chomley by Superintendent Brown, who then forwarded it to the Solicitor General Mr Agar Wynne, along with a request to exhume the bodies of Henry, Elsie and May Needle. The request was approved by Mr Wynne, and the process of disinterment commenced.[94]

When the order was read to Martha, as requested by her, she allegedly said to the Matron 'There is nothing about my youngest child in that order.' The death of this child was not treated suspiciously by the detectives, and in any case the child was buried in a mass grave with other children as an infectious disease had passed through Melbourne at that time. However, such a comment would be used against her in court.

Shortly after, Martha was sent to the city court house to hear the charges against her, and the detectives requested a further remand until 12th July. Mr Keogh, Police Magistrate, asked Martha if she had any objections to the remand, to which she simply replied 'No sir.' Her appearance at this time was reportedly more haggard and worn than in previous public appearances, although she presented calmly.[95] Martha was soon sent back to the female ward of the Old Melbourne Gaol.

---

94   The Argus, 5th July 1894
95   The Argus, 6th July 1894

Henry, Elsie and May were exhumed at the Boroondara Cemetery at Kew, Melbourne on 10th July, 1894. Attending the exhumation of the Needle family were Detective-Sergeant Whitney and Detective Fryer, Mr Neild, Mr J Neild (son), Mr C R Blackett, Government Analyst, Dr Boyd, Mr Branson (Member of the Royal College of Surgeons), Mr Herbert King, undertaker, three grave diggers and two photographers. It was the middle of winter, a bitterly cold and miserable morning with the cemetery thickly veiled in fog.[96] There was no headstone marking the graves, but *The Weekly Times* reported that there was a metal shield which read:

*In Loving Memory of My Dear Children:*

*Mabel, who died Dec 28th 1885, Aged 3 years and 7 weeks*
*Elsie, who died Dec 9th 1890 aged 6 years and 2 months and*
*May, who died August 27th, 1891, aged 4 years and 11*
*months.*

*Little lips that murmured mamma, Still and silent now are they;*
*Tiny feet no longer patter,*
*Hushed forever 'neath the clay.*
*One by one they wandered from me, And I linger here alone;*
*But their sweet and loving mem'ries*
*Blossom through the lonely years.*

*By their loving mother –M.Needle.*

The paper also added that it could be assumed that Martha Needle wrote these lines *'and it will be remembered that her correspondence with Otto Juncken contained several attempts at original poetry of the love-sick order.'*

96   The Argus, 11th July 1894

The examination of the bodies did not occur at the cemetery, but samples of the organs were sent off to the City Morgue and Blackett for examination. The bodies were immediately reinterred on the cold wintery morning.

Martha Needle, circa 1889. Australian Manuscripts Collection, State
Library of Victoria.

May, left and Elsie Needle, circa 1889. Australian Manuscripts Collection, State Library of Victoria.

Martha Needle, circa 1892 (W. Mason & Co, 150 Bridge Rd, Richmond). Australian Manuscripts Collection, State Library of Victoria.

Martha Needle, upon imprisonment in September 1894. PROV. VPRS 516/P0002
Central Register of Female Prisoners 1857 - 1948. (VPRS 516/P0002, Unit 11,
Prisoner No.s 5926 - 6415, Needle Martha: No. 6327, page 409, Year 1894).

THE HOUSE, 137 BRIDGE-ROAD, RICHMOND.

Juncken Saddlery, 137 Bridge Rd, Richmond. Source: The
Weekly Times, 23rd June 1894.

Otto Juncken (Yuncken) in later life. Source:
Hansen Yuncken

Martha Needle's Death Mask, Old
Melbourne Gaol

In preparation for hanging. Picture: Old Melbourne Gaol.

There were said to be only male wardens in the Gaol in Martha's time, although Martha was attended by female wardens in court and a female salvation army worker at the gaol.

Gaunson, David (1846–1909), Obituaries
Australia, National Centre of Biography,
Australian National University,
http://oa.anu.edu.au/obituary/gaunson-
david-3599/text24304

Photo of Alexander Lee which appeared in
the SA Register, 18th June 1920.

# 6

# Melbourne City Police Court Trial

When Martha appeared before the Melbourne City Court on 12th July 1894, for the charges against her to be heard, she was still dressed in 'half mourning', as was custom for the Victorian era. She was wearing a black dress with sealette jacket, a black straw hat with ribbons and an open veil. Etiquette for the traditional mourning period was two and a half years for a husband's death and one year for a child's. There were various stages of mourning: the 'half-mourning' period referred to the last six months of mourning, and was characterised by adding fashionable accessories to clothing, such as ribbons and lace. As it had been over a year since her last child died, she was likely showing mourning for Louis Juncken whom she was convicted of murdering. There were different opinions proffered in the newspapers about Martha's emotional state in court, from having no sign of emotion,[97] to being composed, with traces of anxiety.[98] Whilst Martha was present at the court, as was standard for the accused during this period, she could not directly provide evidence or be questioned.

---

97   The Evening Standard, 14th July 1894
98   The Weekly Times, 14th July 1894

The case drew the curiosity of a large number of Victorians, and particularly women fascinated by the case. It had been over two years since there had been so many women attending the court, the last time when Mr Frederick Deeming was on trial for murdering his second wife Emily Mather, after he had escaped England due to murdering his first wife and four children. The unfortunate Emily had her head cut off and her skull was exhibited at the trial, and later her body was exhumed so that she could be reburied with her head and moved from a pauper's grave to consecrated church burial grounds.

Hearing the charges on the all-male bench were Messrs Keogh, P.M., and Cherry, Lancashire, Andrews, Learmonth and Bird, JPs. Martha was charged first with 'causing to be taken by one Herman Juncken certain poison with intent to kill and murder the said Herman Juncken' and on a second charge with having 'feloniously and wilfully murdered Louis Juncken.'[99]

Mr Charles Finlayson was the barrister who opened for the Crown. He described to the bench the circumstances around the deaths of Louis and the attempted murder of Herman, even though the bench would have been very familiar with the case as every newspaper in the colony had reported on it. Finlayson said that 'Rough on Rats' was found in the Juncken household, and that it would be proven that Martha Needle purchased the packet before Louis fell ill.

Otto was the first witness asked to testify. Finlayson asked Otto how he had met Martha, and he replied that it was at a boarding house in Richmond, kept by Mrs Nicholson, and twice at parties held at the house where the Needles later lived. Some of the newspapers had reported that 'lovesick'

---

99    The Weekly Times, 14th July 1894, The Argus, 13th July 1894

93

Martha and Otto had first met each other in South Australia, adding fuel to rumours and developing upon a motive for Martha to have done away with her husband.

Otto said that about nine months after her husband died, he bumped into Martha on Swanston Street and repeated that she said how she thought it 'unkind that none of his family had come to see her in her trouble.' Otto told of how he was soon visiting Martha and her children regularly.

Otto was torn between his feelings and desire to support Martha daily, through visits and furnishing information to Gaunson, and the stark truth that she could have been responsible for attempting to murder his brother Herman, for murdering his brother Louis, her husband Henry and the poor little children in her own family. He was eagerly keen to hear the reports of evidence. Gaunson took to the floor to cross-examine Otto.

'Up to August 1891, had you noticed anything at all in connection with the state of her health?'

'She enjoyed a fairly good health.'

'By Louis's death, were you likely to gain anything in a pecuniary way?'

'No, I did not.'

'Were you a loser?'

'Yes, my brother was in my debt, and I hold no security.'

Otto described how Martha came to live in the Richmond house, and the Easter when he had gone away with his brothers to Healesville and returned to find Martha quite ill. The aforementioned 'suicide' letter from April, 1892, written by Martha when Otto was on his trip to Healesville, was read out by Otto. This caused a stir among the courtroom, with many women including Martha breaking into tears as the sorrowful words were read out. Otto then went on to describe how he called for Dr MacColl who 'prescribed marriage' as a solution to Martha's unhappiness. Otto told of how coldness developed between Louis and Martha when Martha discovered that Louis had written home to his mother with concerns about the impending marriage.

'Can you account for the change in Louis's character towards her?'

'I think he considered her too violent-tempered a woman to be my wife.'

'Had she manifested violence of temper?'

'Yes.'

'And did it appear to you that there was any occasion for these exhibitions of demeanour?'

'No, we couldn't understand the cause of these violent outbreaks. The occasion did not seem to warrant them.'

'Towards whom did she manifest temper?'

'Towards anyone.'

Otto went on to describe how his mother advised against his impending marriage to Martha due to her ill health. When Otto was re-examined by Finlayson, he described the seizures of Martha, and how they came about suddenly without 'any premonitory sign.' He said that they frequently occurred in the evening, but could occur several times on one day, and lasted for hours during which time her eyes were glazed and wide open, staring into the distance and 'her eyeballs could be touched without effect.' During her fits she was often insensible to pain and was rigid and numb to her body being dragged about when carried upstairs.[100]

Clara Stevens, the nurse who had attended Louis Juncken the day he died, was the next witness. She described how she

---

100 The Argus, 13th July 1894

gave brandy and milk to Louis about twenty times during the afternoon, as prepared by Martha, and that he did not vomit or complain of pain – likely as he was numbed by the alcoholic mixture or exhausted. This was a curious point as vomiting, abdominal pain and diarrhoea and burning of the mouth and throat are key symptoms of arsenic poisoning. Nurse Stevens was cross-examined by Gaunson.

'How was the accused towards Louis Juncken?'

'She was in and out of the room and was very kind and attentive.'

'Have you seen any other cases of poisoning in your time?'

'I have seen cases of blood poisoning, but though in those cases, as in this, the patient was quiet. This case was very unlike the others.' At this stage, Clara appeared faint, and had to be assisted out of the witness box. The case was full of high drama as the accused, witnesses and members of the court broke down through the emotion of it.

The next witness to be heard was Scotsman Dr Donald Stewart MacColl. The doctor was an upright and deeply religious man, a member of the Melbourne Bible Studies group, concerned with telling the truth and keeping his reputation as a medical man, which had been called into question by coroner Dr Neild and Blackett's chemical analysis reports. As per the letter he had sent to the daily newspaper, Dr MacColl believed that he should have been at the coronial post-mortem examination of Louis. The cross examination was an opportunity for him to 'save face' as much as anything, and Gaunson helped the doctor in this regard. Dr MacColl was keen to point out that he had obtained a second opinion, even though he had not performed a post-mortem examination, due to the reluctance of the Juncken family.

Dr MacColl said that he first saw Louis on the 18th August 1893, and diagnosed Riggs' disease of the jaw, but the patient had recovered after a week. Riggs' disease was named after American dentist John Riggs and was the historical term for chronic periodontitis or gum disease and characterised by purulent inflammation of the gum and tooth sockets and the development of pus and loose teeth.[101]

The next time Dr MacColl saw Louis was on 26th April, 1894, and a few days later he was called to the Juncken household. Louis told the Doctor that he felt that he had the same disease as the previous August, and Dr MacColl observed putrid pus emerging from the gums and vomiting. After a slight recovery and washing out the stomach (still a treatment for arsenic poisoning),[102] Louis fell ill again, and 'artificial feeding' (an enema) was introduced. Louis again improved, and feeding by the mouth was again introduced, which was again linked to Louis feeling ill. Dr MacColl said that when examining the heart of Louis, he heard a 'blowing murmur' and concluded that pus had 'been absorbed by a raw patch on the stomach and carried by the circulation to the heart, causing ulcerative endocarditis.'[103] Gaunson cross-examined MacColl.

'You have said that on the morning of the 11th the mouth seemed worse than ever, and that you decided to allow the mouth and stomach to rest?'

'Yes.'

'You reached the house early on that morning. Had he before you got there taken anything to eat?'

---

101  Memidex: http://www.memidex.com/riggs-diseases

102  Encyclopaedia Britannica: https://www.britannica.com/science/arsenic-poisoning

103  Ulceration of the heart valves, associated with infectious or septic disease.

'I was informed that he had taken breakfast that morning.'

'From that time to the morning of his death he was artificially fed?'

'Yes.'

'And on the morning of his death you permitted him to take fluids by the mouth because he seemed better?'

'Yes.'

This point may have laid grounds for suspicion for arsenic poisoning via the 'milk and brandy' mixture prepared by Martha. However, Gaunson suggested that swallowing fluids would have enhanced organic poisoning from the gums – the result of Riggs' disease – to travel down the body.

'The certificate of death which you gave states that, in your opinion, he died from organic poisoning?'

'Yes.'

'Did you discuss the subject of inorganic as well as organic poison with Dr Grant?'

'Yes. We discussed it for about twenty minutes or so, very earnestly, owing to the uniqueness of the symptoms.'

'The conviction impressed upon your mind was that all the symptoms which you had closely observed were consistent with organic poisoning?'

'Yes.'

'And consequently, you gave the certificate of death?'

'Yes, without any hesitation.'

'Does Dr Grant bear the reputation of being an able man?'

'Yes, he is not second to any man in Melbourne.'

'Why?'

'Because he is a gold medallist of Edinburgh University.'

'You ascribed death to the condition of the heart caused by organic poisoning. Therefore, you asked for a post-mortem for the purpose of examining the heart only?'

'That is so.'

Arsenic poisoning mainly affects the kidneys, liver, lung and bladder, but can also lead to cardiac problems including cardiomyopathy and fatty degeneration of the heart.[104] If the other organs of Louis had been examined at the first post-mortem, including the intestine, arsenic poisoning may well have been discovered. Gaunson continued to explore the possibility that Louis died from organic poisoning.

'Would the organs affected by inorganic poisons be the same as would be affected by organic poisons? The stomach and intestines would be affected by such poisons as you believed him to have died from?'

'Yes, or by gastritis arising from any cause.'

'Would congestion of the intestines and stomach be consistent with your theory?'

'Yes. The inflammation of the stomach and other organs would be quite consistent with organic poisoning.'

'The appearances, you say, possibly are consistent with both causes of death?'

'Yes.'

'Were the portions of the body taken away sufficient for an examination on the result of which life and death is to hang?'

'It would be sufficient to determine the presence of poison, but not to determine the cause of death.'

'In the course of your practice, how many cases of arsenical poisoning have you come across?'

'I am glad to say this is the first.'

'Have any of the symptoms that you observed in Louis since arrested your attention as being peculiar to arsenical poisoning?'

---

104  US Agency for toxic substances and disease registry https://www.atsdr.cdc.gov/csem/csem.asp?csem=1&po=11

'No, there was no symptom peculiar to arsenical poisoning except the vomiting, which was not persistent.'

Gaunson paused to reflect to the bench. 'I may tell you very frankly that the case for the prosecution, so far as I can see, rests entirely upon the purchase by the accused of Rough on Rats on May 10th.' He then continued his questioning of Dr MacColl.

'On the following day he vomited again, and his mouth was in a worse condition than ever?'

'Yes.'

'From that time out there was no vomiting whatever?'

'None.'

'Then the symptoms of vomiting, seeing that it only happened once after the purchase of Rough on Rats, was not necessarily of any consequence?'

'I ascribed it to the gum poison. His mouth was worse than ever.'

Gaunson seemed to be satisfied that he had demonstrated that organic poisoning could have been a cause of death, despite the existence of arsenic in the body of Louis. He then turned towards the relationship between Martha and Louis.

'Did you ever see anything in the manner of the accused that was not affectionate and kind?'

'No.'

'Did she, so far as you can judge, give him every attention in Louis's illness?'

'She did. Her manner was very kindly and attentive.'

'Did you at any time observe any flightiness or looseness in her conduct?'

'I have been going to the house for two years, and always thought her conduct most exemplary.'

'And as for Otto Juncken?'

'I thought him one of the most straightforward and noble hearted men I ever saw.'

'Can you say that you either voluntarily or involuntarily had any hand in bringing them together?'

'I attended her for her first illness, and he wanted to know what the matter with her was. This was about April 1892. I said I couldn't make out anything physically the matter with her, but she seemed to have some mental worry, and from something she let drop, I believed it was because her affection was unreciprocated.'

'You put the idea into his head by that sentence?'

'Quite so...I had a very high opinion of Charles, Louis and Otto Juncken. Otto was always very steady and sober.'

Gaunson finished his cross-examination and Dr MacColl was re-examined by Finlayson. Finlayson was keen to highlight that MacColl did not think Martha to be mentally unwell and was a suitable marriage prospect, even though she was clearly deeply troubled, suffering from deep depression and had stated that she would make an attempt on her life. The lack of appreciation for the depth of her suffering was astounding. Finlayson was wary of the 'insanity' plea and keen to undermine any evidence suggesting that Martha was mentally unwell.

'I understand you to say, with respect to Mrs Needle, you say there was no reason why she shouldn't marry, neither mentally nor physically?' asked Finlayson.

'None.'

'You had heard of her having fits?'

'Yes.'

'But as a medical man, you saw nothing in them to prevent marriage, as they didn't affect her mind?'

'Yes.'

Overall, MacColl did not come off well in presenting his evidence. Martha was exposing the failings of both Dr MacColl and Dr Grant, the 'gold medallist from Edinburgh University' and other doctors. Perhaps the Doctor was biased by the strong cultural affiliations they shared in their home country; the Scottish solidarity binding MacColl to Martha may have helped to disguise her true character and show her in a positive light. His evidence also indicated a lack of understanding of depression and any mental disorder that Martha might now be labelled with.

Benjamin Baker, chemist, was called forward to identify prescriptions as copies of originals given by Dr MacColl. This was a period when chemists were frequently investigated, prosecuted and convicted for manslaughter for inappropriately selling (or in one 1895 case in Sydney, even giving away)[105] or overprescribing and overdosing poisons. Under the Poisons Act of the time, it was a requirement for those purchasing a poison to be known to the chemist and for the purchaser to have a witness and sign the chemist's 'poison book' acknowledging receipt of the poison. Extraordinarily, purchasers could easily engage in 'chemist shopping' to obtain the poison they desired – which is what Martha frequently did, as she did with doctors. Baker's was the pharmacy closest to the Juncken household, and while Baker knew Martha and kept Rough on Rats in his pharmacy, she strangely never purchased any directly from him.

Mr Gaunson asked Mr Baker, 'Who usually sells Rough on Rats?'

'Any registered chemist to anyone known to the vendor.'

'The vendor?'

---

105 Weekly Times, Melbourne, 18th October, 1895. 'The Chemist who Supplied the Poison.'

'Yes, I should be the vendor. I know you, Mr Gaunson, and if you came to me I should sell you Rough on Rats.' The courtroom erupted in great laughter.

The questioning continued late into Friday afternoon, when the court adjourned to the following Monday. On Monday, the first witness to be heard was Herbert Streeton, assistant to Benjamin Baker. He testified that he had made up three of Dr MacColl's prescriptions, and Baker one, and none of them had contained arsenic.

Stanley Setford, carpenter, was the next witness. He had boarded at 137 Bridge Road at the time of Louis's death. When he started boarding there, Otto, Louis and Charles Juncken were also residents, along with James Winwood and Martha Needle, and when he left there was only Otto and Martha present. At the time living de facto in an unmarried situation was highly scandalous. Catherine Helen Spence's second novel 'The Handfasted', written in 1880, referred to trial-marriage, via de facto relationships. It was submitted for a prize in 1880 and was rejected as being 'calculated to loosen the marriage tie ... too socialistic and therefore dangerous.'[106] It remained in manuscript form until it was finally published in 1984.

Stanley Setford was asked about relations between Martha and Louis.

'I formed the impression, and I believed it true, that Louis gave her unnecessary work. She said he gave her unnecessary work, but after the first few days she was very kind.'

Setford said that Martha and Louis were 'not on the best of terms,' and after Louis's death she spoke of him as being

---

106  Eade, S. 'Spence, Catherine Helen (1825–1910)', Australian Dictionary of Biography, National Centre of Biography, Australian National University, http://adb.anu.edu.au/biography/spence-catherine-helen-4627/text7621, published first in hardcopy 1976

very selfish. She had also complained of mistreatment by Mrs Juncken and said that she would like to 'give her a dose of poison.' But when Gaunson asked Setford about Martha's treatment of Louis around the time of his illness, he said that she was very friendly to him and nothing aroused suspicion.

George Miller, chemist's assistant at Richards' chemist, then told of how he sold a box of Rough on Rats to Martha on the 10th May, and that she was accompanied by Mr Brittain, a well-known boot salesman who worked for the Exhibition Boot Company in Swan Street, Richmond. Brittain had known Martha for seven years, and she had requested him to accompany her to buy the rat poison. He had instead suggested she use phosphor paste, but she said she had already tried it but that it was ineffective. He locked up the shop and they headed for Richards' chemist on Swan Street, Richmond. Martha had a way with persuading men such as Brittain to do what she wished.

'Did she ask you to take her to Richards' chemist?'

'She mentioned Mr Styles' name, but I told her that as I usually go to Mr Richards, that we should go there.' The cash-strapped Styles chemist was usually willing to sell Martha the poison.

Mr John Jones, brother-in-law to the Juncken brothers, was another witness who testified. He reported that he had stayed at Bridge Road in 1893 and when Gaunson asked Jones whether anything occurred at that time that showed 'strained relations' in the household, Jones replied that he did not.

Finally, it was Herman Juncken's turn to testify. He reported that he stayed at Bridge Road after Louis's death, and asked Martha about Louis's illness. Martha said he had died from 'his heart being affected.' When asked if Louis was conscious or not before his death, Martha said that she was in the room before he died, and that she had spoken to him shortly before his death.

Herman travelled back to South Australia with the coffin, and then when he returned to Melbourne to tidy up his brother's affairs, Martha met him at the station in the morning. Later in the afternoon she took to her bed as she was sick. Herman asked her if there was anything he could do for her, and Martha replied that there wasn't. He asked her if she had any ill feeling towards him, as he felt she thought of him as an enemy.

'You are entirely mistaken. I have nothing at all against you,' she had said.

Herman and Martha had proceeded to talk about Mrs Juncken, and Herman reported Martha saying 'I think your mother has treated me badly. She scarcely spoke to me when she came to the house when Louis died.'

Herman defended his mother, 'She wasn't in a fit state to speak to anybody. Mother later thanked her for her care of Louis and said that there was no ill feeling on her side, and that at such times all should be forgotten. I told Martha that she was to blame for not meeting mother 'in the same spirit."' Herman then advised Martha that she would need to find another 'situation' as a housekeeper, as it would not be right for Otto and herself to live at Bridge Road without being married. Herman then reported that the following morning after breakfast, he fell ill and began to vomit.

Finlayson took up the questioning. 'On the morning of 6<sup>th</sup> June had you breakfast at the Bridge Road house?'

'Yes.'

'Who gave it to you?'

'Mrs Needle. No one else was present. I had a couple of fried eggs and a cup of tea.'

'After breakfast, what occurred?'

'Immediately after breakfast I felt ill, went outside, and vomited. When I came back I told Mrs Needle, and she advised me to go upstairs and lie down. After lying down for a while, I was seized with a second vomiting fit, and took a drop of brandy from a flask that I had brought over with me. Shortly after, I vomited again. Mrs Needle came upstairs and asked whether she could get anything for me. I said I should like a cup of good strong tea, and she went downstairs to prepare it. I followed her shortly afterwards, and drunk the tea.'

'Prior to your breakfast in what state of health had you been?'

'In first-rate health.'

'What did you do afterwards?'

'I went from Bridge Road to the Smith's house, and Dr Boyd was sent for. Next day at noon I went back to Bridge Road and had lunch – a cup of tea and a slice of bread and butter. Almost immediately I fell ill again, and went upstairs to lie down, but only remained there a little time, as the smell of carbolic[107] was too strong for me. I then went back to Smith's, taking nothing further to eat or drink, and then again sent for Dr Boyd. I vomited once after the Doctor's arrival, and this was preserved on advice of the Doctor. During the next two or three days I visited Mrs Needle during the day, and on the 13th I went there from the detective's office. She made a cup of tea for me.'

Finlayson continued, 'While she was preparing the tea, did you stop in the kitchen the whole time?'

'No, I went into the shop two or three times. Once as I was going out, she asked me to go into Miss Howell's, next door, and get a glass of milk, and I did so.'

'You saw her pour out the tea. Did she pour out any for herself?'

'Yes, out of the same pot. She handed me a cup, and I called in the detectives. I took the cup with me.'

---

107 Carbolic soap used for cleaning introduced in 1894, with a strong tar scent.

Gaunson cross examined Herman again about his views on the relationship between Otto and Martha, to try to prove that she had no motive to attempt to murder Herman. 'Did she seem to take your arguments about the desirability of their future relations being somewhat altered, in good part?'

'Yes, she took them in good part, but she did not agree with me.'

'What manner was it of hers that struck you as strange?'

'It seemed reserved, as though she did not care to see me in the house.'

'She said "I have no ill will against you." Did that convey to your mind the impression that she had ill will against someone else?'

'No, I can't say it did.'

'You have heard Mr Setford's evidence, in which he said that the accused said she wouldn't be sorry if the train broke down, and that she would like to give Mrs Juncken a dose of poison. Does that occur to your mind as being stronger or weaker than her letter to Otto?'

'Stronger.'

'Well now she had an opportunity of giving her a dose of poison, hadn't she?'

'I think not.'

'All these observations, verbal and written, have occurred since Otto left Melbourne to go to the funeral?'

'Yes.'

'Doesn't that letter [to Mrs Juncken] read a very cranky sort of letter?'

'I don't know.'

'When did you open communication with the police?'

'On the 13^th of June.'

'But your suspicious had been aroused before?'
'Yes.'
'Dr Boyd attended you on the first day?'
'Yes.'
'You took medicine on that day – did you keep it down?'
'No.'
'When did Otto put a stop to your vomiting by applying a mustard poultice?'
'On the Wednesday evening.'
'He ought to take out a diploma as a medical man,' said Gaunson. The courtroom burst into laughter.
'Did the vomiting continue on the next day – the seventh?'
'No.'
Herman went on to describe how he went to lunch with Martha the next day.
'Did you see the tea made?'
'I paid no attention.'
'You took a cup of tea and a thin slice of bread and butter. Afterwards you felt queer?'
'Yes.'
Gaunson then turned to Martha's role in delaying her marriage to Otto and acknowledging her own sickness.
'Are you aware that Mrs Needle herself desired that her marriage should be put off on the grounds of her health?'
'Yes, from what Otto told me.'
'Then do you come to the conclusion or not that you can see any possible reason or motive for the alleged crime?'
'Well, I have an opinion of course.'
'Was Louis objecting to the marriage?'
'I don't know.'
'Were you?'
'No.'

'Then what motive could she have for pulling you out of the way?'

'I thought it was to spite my mother.'

Gaunson jumped on this comment to suggest Martha's poor mental state. 'Then that's madder than ever. You still think that the motive in her mind was to revenge herself upon the mother by murdering her children? Wouldn't that be a mad thing? It seems most unreasonable. Would it not be the very maddest thing you ever heard of?' insisted Gaunson.

'Yes,' replied Herman.

Concerned at the way Gaunson was directing the conversation, Finlayson quickly rose to ask Herman questions about Martha's mental health.

'Do you see any madness in poisoning your tea and not her own?' Finlayson was trying to establish the wilful intention and awareness of Martha in poisoning Herman's tea only.

'No,' replied Herman.

Gaunson interjected, 'The old wild beast theory of right or wrong.' Gaunson was referring to a principle established for criminal cases in 1723 whereby accused persons, to be able to successfully plead insanity, must prove that they were no more aware than a 'wild beast' of what they were doing, or of what was 'right or wrong.'[108] A similar case from 1843 established

---

108 'The invisible line which it was so difficult to define was not, let it be noted, between sanity and insanity, but between perfect and partial insanity. It was thought no inhumanity toward the defects of human nature to punish as a fully responsible agent a person who was suffering from partial insanity, whatever influence the disease might have had upon his unlawful act.

The principle thus laid down by Lord Hale was subsequently acted upon in English courts. Thus, in the trial of Arnold, an undoubted lunatic, for shooting at Lord Onslow, in 1723, Mr. Justice Tracy said: "It is not every kind of frantic humor, or something unaccountable in a man's actions, that points him out to be such a madman as is exempted from punishment; it must be a man that is totally deprived of his understanding and memory, and doth not know what he is doing, no more than an infant, than a brute or a wild beast; such a one is never the object of punishment." In this respect a wide distinction was

the test for criminal insanity still used today, whereby Daniel McNaughton[109] shot Prime Minister Peel's secretary.[110] The McNaughton rules refer to a defendant having to prove that they suffered a disease of the mind that prevented them from understanding the nature and quality of the act, or if they did know what they were doing that they were unaware that the act was wrong, at the time that it took place.[111] If a crime was committed in secret or with the appearance of rationality (presumably not part of a psychotic episode), then the accused could be perceived to be still fully aware of knowing right from wrong and suffer the full consequence of the law. The McNaughton rule has been criticised for not considering neurological evidence on compulsion and lack of impulse control.[112] There was also the issue of proving that one was suffering from a mental health episode at the time the crime took place, when there was little understanding of mental health and psychiatry was still developing. One alternative to the McNaughton rule is the 'New Hampshire rule' or 'Product rule,' where the test was whether 'the act in question was the "product" of a mental disease or defect.'[113] If the 'Product

---

maintained between civil and criminal cases; for while the law would not allow exemption from punishment for criminal acts unless the reason was entirely gone, it invalidated a person's civil acts, and deprived him of the management of himself and his affairs, when his insanity was only partial, and when the act voided had no discoverable relation to it. A man's intellect might not be sufficient to enable him to conduct his affairs, and to dispose of his property, though quite sufficient to make him responsible for a criminal act: it was right to hang for murder one who was not thought fit to take care of himself and his affairs.' Henry Maudsley, Law and Insanity, 1894.

109  Actually spelled M'Naghten, but spelt here as it is most commonly used.

110  Evans, C. 'Responsibility and criminal law in the late-nineteenth-century British Empire.' The Howard League for Penal Reform, ECAN Bulletin, Issue 23, June 2014.

111  Ibid.

112  Asokan, T.V. (2016). The insanity defense: Related issues. Indian J Psychiatry. 2016 Dec; 58(Suppl 2): S191–S198.

113  Prosono 1994:21, cited in Shea, P. (2001). M'Naghten Revisited -Back to the

rule' had been used, the outcome for Martha may have been very different.

The Magistrate appeared to be impatient with Gaunson's line of questioning, likely as the McNaughton rule was contested at the time, and the Magistrate turned toward whether it was actually Martha who prepared and supplied the poisonous tea. He interjected Gaunson, asking Herman, 'Did you notice anything peculiar in the taste of the tea?'

'Yes, it had a very peculiar taste on both occasions.'

It was towards the end of the day. Magistrate Keogh announced that the hearing would be adjourned for eight days. The court was still awaiting the chemical analyst's full report following exhumation of the deceased members of the Needle family.

Cuthbert Blackett's eagerly awaited report was provided to police 20th July, 1894. This was curiously the same day that *The Argus* broke the news that there was arsenic found in the bodies of Henry Needle and his two children. Thus, the journalists appeared to have open access to the police. Even though Martha was not charged or tried for murdering her husband or children, the evidence that there was poison in their bodies would be considered by the bench in committing Martha. *The Argus* reported that the Crown would, in fact, rest their case upon this new evidence tendered to corroborate the charges already laid.[114] This was in line with a precedent laid down in the grisly Makin case of 1893 from New South Wales. This was a babyfarming case where the judge had admitted evidence regarding the death of a number of other infants, when John and Sarah Makin were tried for the death of one child. The advocates for the accused were unsuccessful in having such additional evidence dismissed.[115]

---

Future? (The Mental Illness Defence A Psychiatric Perspective). Current Issues in Criminal Justice, vol 12, no 3.
114  The Argus, 20th July 1894

The official full report of chemical analyst Blackett was thus provided to the court in the Martha Needle Case.

*Office of the Government Analyst, July 20th, 1894*

*Regina Vs Needle.*

*Report of the exhumed remains of Henry, Elsie and May Needle.*

*On the 10th inst., accompanied by Dr Neild, Detective-sergeant Whitney, and Detective Fryer, I went to the Kew Cemetery, and was present at the exhumation of three coffins containing the remains of Henry, Elsie and May Needle. The coffins after identification were removed to the morgue, and there opened in our presence. Dr Neild handed to me certain portions of the bodies of each, which I put in separate vessels, and carefully labelled. I also had removed samples of the soil taken from under the three coffins; also the sawdust which was on the bottom of Henry Needle's and Elsie Needle's coffin. These were placed in new clean jars. All were removed to my laboratory by myself and Detective Fryer. The parcels (in all nine) were opened by me, and kept under strict supervision. I proceeded at once with the preliminary examination.*

*No 1: Henry Needle's Remains*

*A. Brain – Careful analysis of this organ, which was very soft and converted into adipocere[116], revealed nothing in the shape of poison.*

---

115  The Weekly Times, 25 March 1893, The Makin Case.

116  'a grayish-white postmortem (after death) matter caused by fat decomposition, which results from hydrolysis and hydrogenation of the lipids (fatty cells) that compose subcutaneous (under the skin) fat tissues.' http://www.enotes.com/adipocere-reference/adipocere

B. *The thorax and parts corresponding to the abdominal region – as so little was remaining I removed as much as possible for analysis, washing and macerating the bones with distilled water in a perfectly clean glass dish. This was added to the soft matter,[117] and on analysis found to contain a considerable quantity of arsenic. The flannel shirt found on the skeleton was in a good state of preservation.*

C. *The sawdust taken from under the body contained no arsenic.*

D. *The earth taken from beneath the coffin was found to be free from arsenic.*

*No 2: Elsie Needle's remains*

*These were found to be far advanced in decomposition, adipocere abundant and very alkaline. I followed the same method of analysis as in No 1, and after much care and perseverance detected the presence of arsenic in small quantities.*

E. *Earth from underneath Elsie Needle's coffin was found to be free from arsenic.*

F. *Sawdust taken from coffin immediately underneath the body gave no indications of containing arsenic.*

---

117 It was interesting that there was still 'soft matter' to be found on the bodies of Henry and May. The exhumation of poisoned bodies only commenced from the 1820s, and prior to this it was believed that poisoning led to the quick decay of bodies. Experiments on the effects of poisoning on putrefaction had commenced in Germany on dogs; it was found that putrefaction on poisoned dogs only occurred after 10 days, and the carcasses were largely intact for about eight to ten weeks, after which the soft parts became drier; after three years they were still dry and undecayed. In the case of Henry Needle, he had now been dead for almost five years, Elsie had been dead for just over three and a half years, and May for nearly three years. It could be expected that the bodies were largely dry, if not entirely decomposed.

*No 3: May Needle's remains*

*I cut out the parts pointed out to me by Dr Neild as containing the rectum. I then removed as much as possible of the internal organs. The lungs and intestines were still recognisable, but very soft. The liver still contained what appeared to be biliary matter. The decomposed organs were very alkaline. On analysis I found a considerable quantity of arsenic. The earth from beneath the coffin did not contain arsenic.*

*In each case I have preserved specimens in cubes, & c., to be produced if required. All the chemicals and apparatus used in these investigations were previously proved to be free from arsenic. Each analysis was conducted separately with its own set of materials.*

*(Signed) C.R. BLACKETT.*[118]

When Martha was told of the results of Mr Blackett's analysis in the Melbourne Goal by Detective Whitney, she reportedly said, 'So they found arsenic, did they?'

Detective Whitney replied, 'Yes.'

Martha replied, 'A few more of my friends died lately, and I can give you their names. Would you like their names and information about their burial? It would be useful if you want to dig them up.'[119]

According to Whitney, this was said in a deadpan way, without any irony. It was comments like these that led to observations that Martha was not aware of the seriousness of her predicament and showed inappropriate emotional responses.

---

118 The Argus, 21st July 1894.
119 The Argus, 25th July 1894

After Blackett's findings, the case was further postponed so that detectives could further examine the relationship between Martha and Henry Needle, even though his death was not the subject of the trial and she had not been charged with his death.

On the 26th July, Otto Juncken again wrote to Mrs Owen to coordinate Martha's visitors in gaol, showing his deep tenderness and concern for Martha despite the growing realisation, hard to ignore, that she had murdered his brother Louis, Henry and the children. Several times Martha had asked for her closest friend Eliza Martin whom he also arranged to visit.

> *137 Bridge Rd,*
> *Richmond*
> *26/7/94*

*Dear Mrs Owen,*

*If you should be going in to see Mrs Needle tomorrow will you kindly be there by 11 o'clock as Mrs Martin whom Mrs Needle has several times inquired about, will be there at that time. I have also written to Mrs Gibbons in case she should be going in or as to avoid any chance of mistakes. I saw her at the Court on Tuesday but had no opportunity to speak to her but a friend of mine saw her at the Gaol in the afternoon. She was then fairly well and was evidently keeping up as well as could be expected under the circumstances. I was glad to hear that you went in last Friday I was afraid that no one had gone in that day. Hoping this will find you all quite well.*

*I remain,*

*Your sincere friend*
*Otto Juncken*

When the Police Court case resumed again on 31st July, the focus was again upon the Doctors involved and the causes of death provided for the deceased members of the Needle family. Mr Edward Crocker produced the death certificates of Henry, Elsie and May Needle. He told of the causes of death: for Henry the cause of death was given as 'subacute hepatitis and persistent vomiting, enteric fever and exhaustion due to obstinacy in not taking nourishment.' Elsie Needle was certified to have died from 'gangrenous stomatitis and exhaustion' and May Needle from 'meningitis.'

Dr Charles Alexander Payne, who had attended May Needle, came forward as a witness. He said that the symptoms he noticed pointed to irritation of the brain. Unlike Dr MacColl, he would not stubbornly fight to maintain his reputation by declaring that he was sure of his initial diagnosis. He declared that he had not prescribed arsenic, but that as arsenic had been found in the body of the child, he had changed his opinion as to the cause of death.

Next in line to refute his original diagnosis was Dr George James Hodgson, who was residing in Windsor, Victoria. He said that he had attended Henry Needle in 1889. He similarly stated that he did not prescribe any arsenic, but that as arsenic was found in the body of Henry he had changed his opinion as to the cause of his death. He said that he had attended Elsie Needle[120] and could not remember if there was vomiting in her case, but there was a fetid discharge from the gums, much like had been the case for Louis Juncken. Gaunson asked Dr Hodgson:

---

120  Geelong Advertiser, Martha Needle's Trial. 27th September, 1894

'There was nothing in the demeanour of the prisoner that led you to think she was acting neglectfully or unkindly to her husband or child?'

'Certainly not.'

A friend of Henry Needle's, Owen Humphrey Evans, then came forth to give evidence. He said that he frequently saw Henry and Martha, and that Martha had spoken to him about Henry.

'In 1886 she told me in the course of conversation that she had "made a mistake in marrying Harry" and that she should have married someone else.'

'*You*, I suppose?'

'No. Someone who is at present, "on the other side."'

Mr Finlayson asked, 'Anything else?'

'No, I said, "Harry is a very decent fellow." I don't remember the remainder of the conversation.'

'Do you remember seeing the body of Henry Needle?'

'Yes, I saw it in the house in Cubbitt Street.'

'Was Mrs Needle present?'

'Yes.'

'Did you have any conversation with her about her husband at that time?'

'Yes. About a fortnight after the funeral she called at the house of a Mrs Tutt, where I was residing, and I went with her to the house of a person whom she visited. I waited outside till she came out, and returned with her. During the conversation I expressed my sympathy with her in having lost her husband. She told me that she wasn't sorry he was dead, and that he had left marks of bruises on her when he died. She said also that people in the neighbourhood were talking about her. I said that there was very little people could say about her. She replied, "They complain of me for not having advertised Harry as 'my beloved husband' in the death notice. I did not

117

do so because he was not my beloved husband." She said also that her husband had treated her as an old woman of sixty by not allowing her to attend dances, and that people in the neighbourhood also said that she would marry again and Mrs Needle added "So I would if I had an offer."'

'What kind of a man was Needle constitutionally?'

'Strong – a short, stout, healthy man.'

Mr Finlayson sat down and Mr Gaunson cross-examined. 'I suppose you saw a good deal of Harry Needle,' said Gaunson.

'Yes.'

'Did he knock her about in the presence of people or secretly?'

'I never knew him to knock her about.'

'Did you believe that he left marks of violence upon her?'

'I didn't exactly believe it.'

Gaunson became furious with the witness and began to intimidate him. '*Look here*, Mr Owen Humphrey Evans, did you communicate this cock-and-bull evidence to the detectives or did they ferret you out?'

'They ferreted me out.'

'So far as you know, he was a loving husband, kind, considerate, and affectionate, and never used his hob-nailed boot upon her?'

'Not as far as I know.'

'Did he tell you he had insured his life?'

'No.'

'Or that he intended to make a will?'

'No.'

'Was there anything in the prisoner's manner or conduct to her husband which caused you to think her lacking in her duty?'

'Yes, on one occasion, returning from work with Henry Needle, she was at my house at tea time.'

'She was never in love with *you* was she?'

'Not that I'm aware of. When I returned home and found her at my house I thought she ought to have been at home getting tea ready for her own husband.'

'And you solemnly stand there and quote that as an instance of unkindness?'

'Yes.'

'Then you may get out of the box so far as I am concerned. I don't want to ask you any more questions,' said Gaunson.

Herbert Stretton, chemist's assistant, was the next witness recalled. He was asked about the preparation of certain prescriptions, which contained bismuth, something that Herman had been prescribed in medication.

Gaunson examined the witness. 'Don't you know that there is a particular preparation of bismuth which is the purest form?'

'Yes, it is a liquid.'

'Do you use it?'

'When it is prescribed.'

'Did you as a matter of business, test your subnitrate of bismuth to see whether it was pure?'

'No, if we were to test all the drugs in the shop we should be doing nothing else all day.'

'And of course, chemists never make any mistakes?'

'Well, no-one is infallible.'

'Oh, I don't know about that. It depends on what religion I belong to.' Again, Gaunson had caused the observers at the tense courtroom to break into laugher.

The motive of killing for the insurance money was then explored. Mr Donaldson, secretary of the Australian Widows' Fund Life Assurance Society took to the stand, and explained that Henry Needle's life was insured for £200. Mr James

Ariell next took to the witness box. He explained that as executor to Henry Needle's estate, one third of the insurance money was paid to Mrs Needle upon Henry's death, and other amounts upon the deaths of the two children.

Mr Gaunson, cross-examining, asked, 'Mr Needle, so far as is known, had not left any will?'

'I believe not.'

'And supposing that a woman were engaged in the nefarious plot of taking away a man's life, she might be doing a foolish thing if there were a will?'

'Yes.'

'And for £51 16s 7d Mr Needle was to be taken off? When the child Elsie died, the share would be much more than the £33 5s 8d you paid her?'

'Yes, it would have amounted to £65. We took up the stand that she was not entitled to it.'

'What was the total? I make it out £188 10s 8d. Murder at £60 per head?'

'It would be about that.'

Gaunson dismissed the witness, demonstrating his point that murder at this price seemed absurd.

Rumours had started circulating in the newspapers that Martha Needle had a number of 'amours,' one of whom was now deceased: Thomas Gilroy. Inference was made that Martha had also been responsible for his death. Gaunson decided to put an end to the rumours. The draper James Molony of Swan Street in Richmond was called to the stand. He reported that a cheque for £2 14s 9d was drawn by the executor's company into his account on August 22nd, 1891.

Gaunson asked 'Did you know a man named Thomas Gilroy?'

'Yes. Gilroy worked for me.'

'When did Gilroy leave your service? I have to trouble you because one of the papers has suggested that the accused also caused his death. Did you ever hear of any alleged love passages between the accused and Gilroy?'

'I had it reported to me in the shop that she was "sweet on him."'

'Did Gilroy take ill in your shop?'

'On a Monday shortly before his death he told me that he felt very unwell, and asked to get off for the day. I think it was in the month of December, 1892. He died on the following Monday.'

'Did you know that at that time the accused was in Adelaide?'

'No.'

'Wouldn't it be surprising if she were that she could have caused his death?'

'I don't know anything about it.'

'And you heard it reported that she was "sweet" on him, or he on her?'

'They were sweet on each other, I heard.'

'Had you heard that Gilroy had ceased visiting at the accused's house for months and months before he was taken ill?'

'No.'

'Had you ever seen them in company?'

'No, except when she came into the shop to make purchases.'

The witness was then dismissed and the court again adjourned to the next morning.

*

On 1<sup>st</sup> of August, Otto Juncken again wrote to Mrs Owen, very keen to ensure that she not communicate to people from Adelaide the fact that he was paying for Gaunson to defend Martha.

> *137 Bridge Rd Richmond*
> *1/8/94*

*Dear Mrs Owen,*

*I am writing to send you the address of Mrs Bowie and Mrs Gondie. I will not trouble Mr Jarvis to transact any business or anything on my account in connection with this unfortunate affair, as I think I will have plenty of time and can do all I want to do by letter. I do not know whether Mr Jarvis is aware of the position I have taken up in the case. I mean as regards paying Mr Gaunson. Possibly he is and I would like you to ask him if he will kindly not mention that fact to the Adelaide folk, they are very fond of gossip over there and I am afraid that should my Mother get to hear it, it will be a great source of trouble to her. You will quite understand my object in mentioning this and I do not wish Mr Jarvis to think that I regard him as a gossiper, only I thought it as well to mention it, he may have in the ordinary course of conversation spoken of it over there.*

*Trusting this will find all of you in good health and that Mr Jarvis will have a most enjoyable trip.*

*I am*
*Your Sincere friend*

*Otto Juncken*

When the court case commenced again the next morning, Mr Greenwood Holt, agent for the Temperance General Mutual Life Association, which had insured the Needle children, gave a statement to the court. He said that he had visited the Needle house every week, had frequent opportunities of seeing the children, and that they were always nice and clean, and that from him there was absolutely no ground for being suspicious towards Martha.

Hannah Tutt, boarding house keeper, was next to give her testimony. 'I have known the accused and her husband since 1885. After Henry Needle's death, I consoled Mrs Needle. She said to me that she was not sorry that he was dead, as he had never been too good to her and had ill-used her. She said that when he was sick he was very stubborn and would not take food. She said also that she had asked him to make a will, and that he had refused.'

Gaunson asked, 'Were you surprised to hear that Henry Needle had misused the accused?'

'Yes, I had not seen him ill-use her.'

The next witness was Martha Needle's childhood friend, Mrs Eliza Martin, and possibly the person who knew her best. She moved up to the witness box to answer Finlayson's questions.

'I have known Martha Needle since childhood,' she stated.

'Did she complain of her husband's unkindness?' asked Finlayson.

'She complained frequently of her husband's unkindness, and I have seen him knock her about.'

There was a murmur through the courtroom.

'What was her relationship to Louis Juncken?'

'She said that Louis Juncken was unsocial and took no notice of her. She also said that she would kill Mrs Juncken if she had to walk all the way to Lyndoch to do it.' Again, there were murmurs and gasps through the courtroom.

'What do you know about the accused's family?'

'I knew Martha's mother, Mrs Foran of Adelaide when Martha was a child of 11 years of age. The Forans were poor, and Mrs Needle went out early to service. At 17 she was married to Henry Needle.'

Mr Gaunson approached the witness box, 'Did you ever see Needle ill-treat her?'

'I have seen him strike her several times. I saw him strike her open-handed over the nose. He also struck her on the side with a piece of deal[121] just before Elsie was born...She told me that he had ill-treated her on another occasion, and caused a miscarriage. She said that he was always cruel, and was always giving her sly thumps.'

'During one of her fits she appeared to be talking to her husband and children, and said to her husband, "You will hit me once too often, Harry Needle."'[122]

'Did you ever see how she was toward her children?'

'I saw Elsie once or twice during her illness. Mrs Needle was always kind to her children and very proud of them.'

She continued, 'Mrs Needle came to the house late one night in a very wild condition, and said that she was going to Kew.'

'To Kew?'

'To the cemetery.'

'What for?'

'To see the children's grave. Then she went into a fit. On another occasion she came to my house and complained of dreadful pains, and called out, 'Oh, my head. I'm silly,' and

---

121  Fir or pine board.
122  Geelong Advertiser, The Richmond Poisoning Cases, 2nd August 1894.

fell down. The fit lasted for three or four hours. Her limbs were quite rigid, and one hand was clasped in her hair.'

'Did the stiffness resemble that of after death?'

'She looked just like marble.'

'There was no make believe or gammon[123] about them, was there?'

'Oh no, I think not. Mrs Needle had been subject to these fits ever since her marriage, and several had occurred at the house in Cubitt Street. As a rule, she did not talk in her fits, but on one occasion she said something about the children. Mrs Needle was always kind to her children, and brought them up so as to be a credit to any woman.'

'How do you account for Mr Needle's brutality to her?'

'She told me that he was very jealous of her.'

'Did you ever hear in Adelaide that any attempt was made to poison Mrs Foran at any time?'

'Never.'

'You said she had fits?'

'Mrs Needle said to me once, 'Oh, these pains in my head. They will either kill me or drive me mad.'

At this point Mr Finlayson expressed his desire to re-examine the witness.

'What was the name of her mother?' asked Finlayson.

'The name of the supposed mother of the accused was Mary Foran. In Adelaide, Mrs Needle was called Mattie Charles. Mrs Foran had two sons — Daniel and John Foran. They were Mrs Needle's stepbrothers.'

Eliza Martin was finally asked to step down from the witness box and Mr Robert Robinson, railway ganger living at Morwell (Gippsland), and a friend of the

---

123 Gammon/gammin: joking or acting, pretending.

Needles, stepped up. He was a former neighbour, with his wife and family.

'How long have you known the accused?' asked Finlayson.

'A little over nine years.'

'What were the terms of their relationship?'

'So far as I could tell, Mr and Mrs Needle lived on very good terms. Later on, I saw Mrs Needle in Adelaide, and she complained of her husband's treatment of her. She said that he accused her of some impropriety with a man in the house.'

'When did you last see Needle?'

'I visited Henry Needle during his last illness, and on the night before the death Mrs Needle told him that her husband's illness would be fatal, as Dr Singleton visited him at her request a day or two earlier, and said that he could not live.'

'After Henry Needle's death I went to live at Morwell, and I was visited there by Mrs Needle. When I asked if she "Wouldn't be glad if Harry were alive?" she said "No, I would not. If he walked in through that door I wouldn't speak to him."' There were gasps in the court as Finlayson retired from questioning. The witness was cross-examined by Gaunson.

'Did Harry Needle speak to you about Singleton's visit?'

'I had several conversations with Mr Needle during his illness but he never said anything to me about Dr Singleton having seen him. Mrs Needle told me that Dr Singleton had asked Harry whether he was prepared to die, and that he had answered "No Sir." Mrs Needle's brother was present during the illness.' He must have been referring to John Foran, as Daniel Foran junior had lost touch with the family from the time he went to the Magill Industrial School as a child.

'We are told that Needle was jealous.'

'I had reason to believe so.'

'Was it specific or general?'

'I think it was of a general character.'

'Do you remember a man named Altmann?'

'Yes, he was jealous of Altmann. There was another man named Mercer about whom he was jealous.'

'Did Needle ever tell you his opinion about his wife's character?'

'Yes, I put the question point-blank whether he thought her guilty of misconduct with any man. He said "no."'

'Did Needle tell you that he watched his wife?'

'He told me that he came down to Melbourne in consequence of an anonymous letter from a woman, whom he believed to be Mrs Altmann, and that he had asked Mrs Altmann about the letter. She admitted the authorship and said that the statements were true. Henry Needle said that he had then spoken to his wife, who said that Mr Altmann had visited the house, but denied any impropriety.'

'Do you remember one Saturday night your going to the theatre with your wife and Mrs Needle, and going into her house for supper on your return, when Needle came in like a madman, expecting to find Altmann?'

'We had been to Burnley to see a friend, not to the theatre. Needle came in and seemed dumbfounded at seeing us there. Mrs Needle always seemed kind to her husband. She seemed, however, to think that he was not trying to please her. During Needle's illness the accused seemed most kind and attentive; and she was always thoughtful for the children. Until a few days before his death, Needle did not seem to think his illness serious. He complained of a sore throat and mouth which prevented him from swallowing his food. I never saw him vomit.'

Georgina Lillis was the next witness. She said that she had known Mrs Needle for about three years, and at one time lived at Bridge Road. She had heard Mrs Needle complain after Louis

Juncken's death, that Mrs Juncken did not treat her properly. Gaunson asked Lillis more about the fainting fits.

'I looked after the house for about six weeks while Mrs Needle was ill, and noticed that she suffered from fainting fits. I noticed that she suffered from repeated fainting fits and very often she would fall down on the floor and appear like one dead. On the first time that she had these faints, I ran down to Louis Juncken, who told me not to be afraid and said that Mrs Needle was often seized with these fits, and that she ought to be put to bed. Sometimes there would be two fits in one day. They occurred one after the other, at all times. I have known her to fall against the stove, and sometimes she would hurt herself.'

'Did they seem genuine fits?'

'The attacks seemed perfectly real. There was no appearance of simulation about them. In some of these fits she rambled about her children, calling out "Elsie" and "May" as if they were alive, and she always spoke about them in the most endearing terms. She used to walk about in a dazed condition. Mrs Needle had another illness in the same year and went under some slight operation. Her illness lasted over two months. During the whole time she was subject to frequent attacks of fainting, which lasted from 10 minutes to an hour.'[124]

The last witnesses included the detectives working on the case, Dr Neild who performed the autopsies and Blackett, the government analyst.

Detective Whitney noted, 'After she had been committed to gaol, Otto Juncken had applied for permission to send her meals. His request had been referred to the governor of the gaol. During the court proceedings, I had supplied her with

124 The Argus, 27th September 1894

her dinner daily at the request and expense of Otto Juncken.' She had earlier been refused meals being taken to her when she was in the Watch House.

Blackett confirmed the amount of arsenic found in the samples he had analysed, and with his report Blackett was dismissed and the case for the crown concluded. It was quickly decided that the case warranted a full Supreme Court hearing. Magistrate Keogh asked Martha if she had anything to say before committal.

'No' was Martha's firm reply.

Martha Needle was duly committed for trial at the Supreme Court on 15th August.

On 2nd of August, Otto again wrote to his good friend Mrs Owen, and told of Martha's expectations of a positive outcome from the court case.

*137 Bridge Road*
*Richmond*
*2/8/94*

*Dear Mrs Owen*

*If you intend going in to see poor Martha tomorrow will you try and be there at 2.30. I am writing also to Mrs Gibbons and to a Mr Mackney to the same effect and it would be as well if you would arrange among yourselves as to when you will go in again. I had a good talk with her today and she seems hopeful yet that all will come right. Poor girl.*

*With kindest regards to all of you. I am*
*Yours Sincerely*

*Otto Juncken*

After nearly two weeks of waiting for the Supreme Court trial, on 15<sup>th</sup> August, it was announced that the case would not be tried during the August sitting. Gaunson required further time to prepare for his defence of the case. The Crown Law Department did not oppose the request made to and granted by the Chief Justice of the court.

# 7

# Martha Needle's Supreme Court Trial

On 12<sup>th</sup> September it was announced that Martha Needle's trial would commence later that month. It was said that 'Mrs Needle is quite well in the gaol, and still maintains a very great reserve of manner.' The Supreme Court Trial commenced on 24<sup>th</sup> September, when Martha was charged with the death of Louis Juncken in the case 'Regina vs Needle.'

The first business was to select the twelve jurors. Martha would face an all-male jury, as women jurors were not introduced until the 1920s (with Queensland being the first state to introduce women jurors in 1924). Many of the jury would have been well-acquainted with *The Richmond Poisoning Case*, as it was a main feature of all of the daily newspapers. Nevertheless, before the first witness was invited to the witness box, Finlayson for the Crown addressed the jury at length, detailing the history of the case. He elaborated upon the motive for murder as being Louis's disapproval of his brother Otto marrying Martha.

'The fact that Louis was an obstruction to the marriage of Otto and the prisoner was hardly a sufficient motive for murder, but, however extraordinary it might appear, it will be found, from the actions of the prisoner, that it was quite sufficient motive for her,' said Finlayson.

Finlayson read aloud to the court the letter Martha had written to Otto after his brother's death, emphasising the incriminating passage:

> *But remember this, that if you do cast me off for your mother you will soon be motherless. I shall kill her, if I have to walk every mile from here to Lyndoch. I have vowed to my God to do this, and I shall keep my vow. You may think I shall not keep my word and kill her if she parts us. I have quite made up my mind to this: she shall never cause another woman the misery she has brought me.*

Finlayson went on to describe how, when Otto returned to Melbourne after Louis's funeral, he told Martha that he felt it best that they live separately for a time, and that he would not marry without his mother's and brother's consent. Shortly after Herman also suggested that Martha and Otto live separately as it was not the appropriate thing for an unmarried couple to live together, due to 'impropriety,' he suddenly became ill.

Otto was the first witness to be called. He told the court he would often see Martha rigid on the floor, in an unconscious catatonic state which she remained in 'for four or five hours at a time.' When she apparently regained consciousness, she would have amnesia and not recognise anyone around her:

'She would take up some incident from her past and go through it...it appeared as though her mind had gone back to the past and she would apparently be conversing with someone who had been present in the past.'

Otto was frequently confused for one of these people. When Martha was in an unconscious state, Martha would address him as her late husband Henry, and 'she would put up her hand as if warding off a blow.' She would also look around the house for her deceased children and try to leave the house in this fragile state, which Otto would try to prevent, sometimes unsuccessfully. Otto reported that Martha would take a pillow and caress it as if it were one of her dead children.

'It was in conscience of what the Doctor said that I engaged myself to the accused.'

Finlayson asked Otto whether he thought the accused guilty.

'I am of the opinion that if the facts should point that the accused did murder my brother, she was not responsible as she did not know what she was doing.'[125]

Otto was asked about his relationship with Martha. He said that he did not have an intimate relationship with her before May 1892 or before Martha moved into the Bridge Road household. However, the newspapers would report otherwise. He said that he knew that Martha was subject to fits of 'hysteria' and that she had been attended to for typhoid fever and a pain in her side[126] but he had not known that she consulted 'medical men' about her 'fits'. He had found her on two occasions lying on the floor with her hand in a pool of blood, and he believed that she had attempted to take her own life. Otto also reported how they had initially been peaceful together, but she had refused to marry as she was in bad health, suffering from piles and undergoing operations for the condition. Martha threatened to end her life if she was not cured.

Otto admitted that he lent her £3 when her daughter May had died and when she visited Adelaide in 1891. He was also

125  State Library of Victoria, Martha Needle papers, MSS 8296
126  Typhoid can lead to delirium and kidney failure.

asked if he knew there was a box of Rough on Rats purchased on May 10<sup>th</sup>: he said he was unaware of the fact. He revealed that he had previously thrown away a box of Rough on Rats and chlorodyne when he realised that Martha had suicidal thoughts and intentions.

The examination of Otto took almost two hours. Before Gaunson's cross-examination, Justice Hodges spoke sternly to the courtroom observers who were staring at Martha, much to her chagrin.

'I have noticed that some of the persons who are in the seat in front of the dock turn around occasionally to look at the prisoner, and I must request them not to do so. The prisoner is placed in a position of great peril, and her mind ought not to be disturbed by persons staring at her. If what I have observed is repeated, I will have these persons removed from court.'

Dr MacColl was the next witness, and he largely repeated his evidence of the police court trial, telling of how he first attended Louis in August 1893 for 'Riggs Disease of the jaw,' and that Dr Grant initially thought that Louis was suffering from organic poisoning. It is strange to think that poor mouth hygiene and gum disease could lead to an early death, but there is now some evidence for an association between poor oral health and earlier death,[127] although not a quick death as in the case of Louis Juncken. However, this link was not known in the 19<sup>th</sup> century and Dr MacColl now swallowed his pride and, given the evidence, was forced

---

127 Abnet et al., (2005). Tooth loss is associated with increased risk of total death and death from upper gastrointestinal cancer, heart disease, and stroke in a Chinese population-based cohort, International Journal of Epidemiology, Volume 34, Issue 2, 1 April 2005, Pages 467–474. Joshy et al. (2016). Is poor oral health a risk marker for incident cardiovascular disease hospitalisation and all-cause mortality? Findings from 172 630 participants from the prospective 45 and Up Study, BMJ Open, 2016; 6(8): e012386.

to admit that arsenic poisoning was the probable cause of death, but he persisted in saying that there were no clear symptoms of such poisoning.

'I have a large practice in the course of which, this is the first case I have come across of arsenical poisoning. I did not come across it in my student days. There were no symptoms of arsenical poisoning except the vomiting which was not persistent.'

Again, MacColl attested that he did not find Martha's behaviour suspicious, and that she had acted towards Louis in a kind and attentive manner. Curiously, the doctor did not make the connection between the 'fainting fits' where Martha raved about her deceased children and re-enacted scenarios with her deceased husband, and her having an unsound mind.

'I had heard she had fits, but so far mentally I thought it did not affect her mind. If I had seen anything of the accused's manner to the patient being suspicious, I would not have given that certificate.'

The Judge scribbled down some notes which indicated that he was not completely satisfied with the evidence and coronial inquiry, and remarking that one of the doctors involved in the case has experience of working in a lunatic asylum.

*Have read Neild's evidence. Disease of the Jaw in 1894. How does Riggs' Disease of the jaw show itself?' I believe every organ in the body should be examined. Browne (Police Detective) should have been examined... X been in Lunatic Asylum in Glasgow. Prisoner desired a nurse around the beginning of his illness.*

Nurse Clara Stevens presented her evidence the following morning. She confirmed that it was Martha Needle who prepared the milk and brandy that went with the medicine prepared for Louis Juncken. The Judge also noted in his scribblings that 'MacColl gave him a dose himself before his death.'

Stanley Setford then gave evidence, largely repeating his evidence of the Melbourne City Police Court Trial, before Thomas Brittain took the stand. He had changed workplaces and was now a boot salesman at Foy and Gibsons, in Smith Street, Collingwood. He again described how Martha had wanted to go with him to the Styles Chemist, which she regularly went to, but he had refused. Mr and Mrs Styles had both taken their own lives since the commencement of Martha's court trial. Perhaps the trial had given them a great deal of negative publicity, or they had felt in some way partly responsible for the deaths in the Needle family including the small children. Aside from this, Victoria was still feeling the effects of the economic depression and the Styles chemist may have been financially struggling.

Next Herman Juncken was presented as a witness, and he also repeated his evidence of the police court trial. He emphasised that Martha was dissatisfied with his mother's treatment toward her. Martha had said that Mrs Juncken treated her very cruelly. He described again how the morning after he had told her she would have to find 'a situation,' after serving him his two eggs and tea, he had become ill.

'I know of no circumstance to lead me to believe the prisoner had any personal ill-will towards myself. The only conclusion I can come to is that she had an idea that by taking my life and that of Louis she could injure my mother. I can imagine no other reason,' said Herman. 'Some time in June, Mrs Needle wrote to me, evidently relying on me as a friend. That would be between the time Otto wrote to mother saying he was going to marry, and the time of Louis's first illness –between May and August.'

Gaunson then turned towards the point of whether Martha Needle had attempted to prevent the course of justice.

'Mrs Needle made no objection to giving Whitney her keys for the purposes of the search. She burst out crying when they were searching amongst articles of children's clothing and toys which were there, and asked the detectives not to touch them as they belonged to her dead children. Her distress appeared to be genuine, and I was somewhat affected by it,' said Herman.

'When I saw her in bed sick, and spoke to her about living apart from Otto, that was simply to save scandal, and not with a view of separating them. I considered their marriage was a thing for themselves to decide.'

'Did you consider the faint she had on that occasion genuine?'

'No, I did not consider the faint on that occasion to be genuine.'

One of the jury members spoke up to ask Herman about the pain he felt when vomiting.

'I suffered no pain, simply an empty, nauseating feeling,' said Herman.

When Dr Neild was next presented as a witness, he was put to the test by Gaunson due to some inconsistencies reported in evidence on the case.

'Did you send the heart of Louis Juncken on to Mr Blackett?' asked Gaunson.

'No,' replied Neild.

'If Mr Blackett says he received the heart, is he wrong?'

'If he says he received the heart I am sure he is right, but I have no recollection of doing so.'

Dr Neild gave a rich and overly detailed description of the appearances of the exhumed bodies, during which Martha was visibly emotional and 'seemed on the point of fainting.' She was led out of the court, and given a 'restorative' before she recovered and re-entered the court room.

Mr Gaunson resumed, 'You say you did not take the heart away from the cemetery?'

'I say I have no recollection of doing so. My recollection is that, in Juncken's case, I placed the stomach in a separate jar. If Mr Blackett says that the jar contained stomach and intestines, he will be right.'

'It is on the accuracy of your recollection, especially as to the stomach, that this poor life depends.'

'I know that as well as you do, Mr Gaunson. You are merely elocuting.'[128] He was speaking about the contemporary dramatic practice of reading out stories and pieces from plays, bringing fame to the likes of South Australian actress and British suffragist Muriel Matters and other stars of the time. This statement brought the famous rile of Gaunson to the fore.

'I am afraid it is you who is elocuting. Is it true that you put the intestines in a jar with the stomach?'

'My recollection is that I placed the stomach in a separate jar. It was the redness of the stomach and intestines that led me to the conclusion that the cause of death was arsenic; but all I say is that the appearances were consistent with a death from an irritant poison, that irritant poison being arsenic.'

Mr Justice Hodges asked 'Do medicinal doses ever cause death?'

'Not as far as I know,' said Dr Neild.

'Not so far as I know...' repeated Justice Hodges out loud. 'Are you aware that application was made for some medical

---

128 Speaking as if practicing elocution.

men to be sent over to attend the post-mortem on behalf of the prisoner?' asked the Judge.

'I was told so.'

'And it was not done?' asked Hodges.

'No.'

Gaunson then resumed, raising the issue of the coroner speaking directly to the press at the post-mortem even before his report and that of the government analyst were complete. This would not be permitted today, but at the time the coroner spoke freely to the press and they appeared to have free rein over what was reported. Gaunson tried to convey to the jury that newspaper reports would have led to the bias of witnesses, including Dr Neild himself. The judge appeared to want to stop Gaunson following this line of inquiry, because it may have opened a can of worms, with most of the evidence in the case having previously been published in newspapers across Australia and the Tasman sea to New Zealand.

Gaunson asked Dr Neild, 'After the post-mortem, did you have an interview with a representative of the *South Australian Register* newspaper?'

'What is the object of this question?' asked Judge Hodges. 'The jury don't want to know something he said to a reporter, but anything you want to know from Dr Neild, you can ask him.'

'The object will be manifest in this way...'

'I will stop this now in order to prevent further discussions. What the witness said to the reporter has nothing whatever to do with the case.'

'With great respect I ask your Honour to hear me.'

Gaunson had crossed the line with the well-known cantankerous judge.

'No, I will rule it out, and have done with it. It has nothing to do with the case.'

Gaunson persisted, 'I submit that it has to do with the case. Suppose I want to put an argument to the jury that an expert has delivered himself of an opinion which has been published in a newspaper, and that his mind – as even the mind of an honest witness might be – is biased in the direction of supporting in the witness box by his testimony that which he has already stated to a newspaper reporter in connection with this case. Surely that might be a reasonable argument to the jury?'

'As I have told you, you can cross-examine Dr Neild, but you cannot start by reading a report of something that is said to have been said by Dr Neild to some reporter in some part of the world. If Dr Neild gives evidence which varies from what he has previously said, you may cross-examine him as to that statement.'

After some minutes of further cross examination, the dogged Gaunson returned to the subject of the press interview.

'Will you kindly obey the ruling of the court?' said Justice Hodges. 'You can ask his opinion now, and if it varies from what he said previously, you can cross-examine him,' said Hodges.

'Is it your opinion that those appearances might be produced by the ordinary disease of inflammation of the bowels?' asked Gaunson.

'Not the whole of them.'

'Did you ever say to anyone that those appearances might be so produced?'

'No, I did not – not the whole of those appearances. When I was interviewed by a gentleman from the newspaper...'

Hodges interrupted, 'That will do. You need not go into that.'

Gaunson continued, 'Did you find anything to tell you absolutely the cause of death?'

'Not until I knew the result of the analysis.'

'Then your opinion is formed by what you have seen and by the evidence of the analyst taken together?'

'My decided opinion is based on the two combined.'

'Has arsenic any taste?'

'No, not so far as I am concerned, and I have often tried it.'

Finlayson re-examined and again asked about the taste of arsenic.

Dr Neild replied, 'Rough on Rats is, I understand, arsenic mixed with soot, and that would give it a distinct taste. If ten grains of arsenic were dissolved in a cup of tea it might taste the tea, but the taste would be caused rather by the substance with which it was mixed than by the arsenic itself.'

Dr Neild was then asked by Finlayson to inspect the jars containing the body parts sent for analysis. He then backed down from his previous statement to Gaunson.

'I now find that I did include the heart, which was put in a jar with one of the lungs, and I find that the stomach was included with the intestines in one jar. I remember now that that was done because the stomach contained no fluid, and it would make no difference to include it with the intestines.'

The government analyst, Cuthbert Robert Blackett, was next invited to the witness box.

'How much arsenic did you find in the bodies of the deceased?' asked Finlayson.

'From analysing 80g of stomach and intestine of Louis Juncken, I calculated that there were 3.399 grains[129] of arsenic. The quantity of arsenic sufficient to cause death is from 2 to 2 ½ grains. In the tea given by the prisoner to Herman Juncken there was 10 grains of arsenic. From the

---

129  1 grain of arsenic is equivalent to 0.065 of a gram.

remains of Henry Needle, there was 1.4 grains of arsenic. From the child Elsie an infinitesimal trace of arsenic and from those of May, 2.81 grains of arsenic.'

Estimations of the range of acute lethal dose of arsenic vary: from 22 to 300 milligrams[130] [131] [132] of arsenic/kilogram for an adult, and less for a child. It is stated that 'levels between 0.1 and 0.5 mg/kg on a hair sample indicate chronic poisoning while 1.0 to 3.0 mg/kg indicates acute poisoning.'[133] The dose of 3.399 grains of arsenic that was found in Louis Juncken was equivalent to 220 milligrams (in just 80g), in the high range of an acute lethal dose. In Henry's remains there were 90 milligrams, and in May's remains there were 182 milligrams. In Herman's tea, there was an astonishing 647 milligrams of arsenic. But there were only 'infinitesimal' amounts of arsenic in the remains of Elsie – did she actually die from 'gangrenous stomatitis' from living in poor socioeconomic circumstances?

Gaunson asked Blackett about absorption of arsenic from sources such as wallpaper. He raised a very important point that was virtually dismissed by the court. It was only in the 1890s that the true effects of wallpaper were being discovered. Arsenic vapour (usually arising from layer after layer being plastered on) could in fact be diffused into the air of a room especially when damp, and thereby be absorbed; the main culprit being a paint colour popular in Victorian times, called Scheele's Green, especially in the favoured designs of William Morris.[134] The

130  https://www.atsdr.cdc.gov/toxprofiles/tp2-c3.pdf
131  Dart, RC (2004). Medical toxicology. Philadelphia: Williams & Wilkins. pp. 1393–1401.
132  Schoolmeester WL, White DR. Arsenic poisoning. South Med J 1980;73:198–208.
133  R N Ratnaike, Acute and chronic arsenic poisoning. Review. Postgraduate Medical Journal. BMJ Journals. Volume 79, Issue 933 https://pmj.bmj.com/content/79/933/391
134  Ball, P. (2003). William Morris made Poisonous Wallpaper. Nature. 12th June

average room could contain up to 30,000mg of arsenic, sufficient to kill over 100 people.[135] Arsenic was also found in the material used to make prams for babies and in children's toys, along with bread, food colouring, beauty products, soap, medicines, decorative hair products and clothing and pesticides.[136] Inorganic arsenic is still currently used in timber treatments[137] in Australia and in food preparations from other countries, mainly seafood products (at a low level).[138] Arsenic was likely to be abundant in the timber that Henry Needle worked with as a carpenter. In one famous case in 1862, a Dr Thomas Orton had discovered that four children had died from arsenic poisoning that they had come into contact with via Victorian wallpaper in a bedroom.[139] Suspicion over the childrens' deaths was dismissed by a jury, although the case was highly controversial at the time.

Gaunson then seemed to jump from topic to topic, without fully exploring the issue of arsenic or elaborating, perplexing the jury.

'There is such a thing known as post-mortem imbibition or absorption of arsenic. It is indisputable that arsenic can

2003. https://www.nature.com/news/2003/030612/full/news030609-11.html; Hawksley, L. (2016) Could this Wallpaper kill you? The Telegraph, 7th October 2016. https://www.telegraph.co.uk/books/what-to-read/could-this-wallpaper-kill-you-victorian-britains-lethal-obsessio/

135 Arsenic in Wallpaper. Flanders Health Blog. 15th December 2016. http://www.flandershealth.us/lead-poisoning/arsenic-in-wallpaper.html

136 Rae, H. When Poison was Everywhere, The Atlantic, 11th October 2016, https://www.theatlantic.com/health/archive/2016/10/the-era-when-poison-was-everywhere/503654/

137 APVMA Arsenic timer treatments: Chemical Review. https://apvma.gov.au/node/12366

138 FSANZ (2017). Arsenic. http://www.foodstandards.gov.au/consumer/chemicals/arsenic/Pages/default.aspx

139 The Smithsonian Magazine, Arsenic and Old Tastes Make Victorian Wallpaper Deadly, 3rd April 2017: https://www.smithsonianmag.com/smart-news/victorian-wallpaper-got-its-gaudy-colors-poison-180962709/; Hawksley, L. (2016) Could this Wallpaper kill you? The Telegraph, 7th October 2016. https://www.telegraph.co.uk/books/what-to-read/could-this-wallpaper-kill-you-victorian-britains-lethal-obsessio/

be imbibed from wallpaper. If arsenic entered the body, no matter how, the symptoms are the same,' said Blackett.

'Have you heard of Taylor[140] describing cases where stuffed birds have been the cause of arsenic poisoning?' asked Gaunson.

'No, I have not heard of such cases, but if Taylor said so, I would believe it.'

'Have you heard of cases where the effects of bismuth are similar to the effects of arsenic?'

'If authorities said that the effects of bismuth on the stomach were the same as those of arsenic, it was a very extraordinary statement.'

'Do you know anything about the wallpapers in the house at Bridge Road?'

'No, I do not.'

It is strange that this point was not laboured over more, given the high degree of arsenic in daily products of the time. Gaunson turned to the fact that there was not a second opinion provided in the case.

'Are you aware that in trials in the old country, more than one analyst is employed?'

'Sometimes that is so.'

'Is it not in the majority of cases?'

Judge Hodges interrupted, 'How could the witness know that except by what he has heard or been told?'

Berated, Gaunson moved on. 'Is there any taste in arsenic?'

'It has a slightly sweetish taste.'

The hearing was closed for the day after Blackett's evidence. The next morning when the trial resumed, the focus of questions turned to Martha's physical and mental health.

---

140  Likely referring to Taylor's Manual of Medical Jurisprudence, first published 1866. https://archive.org/details/manualofmedicalj00tayl

Mrs Hannah Tutt, restaurant keeper, was the first witness called. She had hardly known the Needle family, especially Martha and the children, yet she spoke with some authority.

'I knew the late Henry Needle, who boarded with me for about three months in 1886[141] upon his arrival in the colony from Adelaide. He was alone then. He then went to Wellington Street, Richmond with his wife and children, Mabel and Elsie being with them. I visited them once at Richmond when May was born. They were healthy, strong children.'

'Were you aware that the youngest child, May, had suffered from marasmus?'[142]

'No, I was not aware of that. The children were nicely, cleanly and tenderly kept. I could not say I ever saw children kept more nicely. I never saw any unkindness.'

'Did you ever see the prisoner after the death of Henry Needle?'

'I only saw the prisoner once, about a fortnight after Henry's death. I only saw the prisoner about half a dozen times altogether.'

The revelation that May had marasmus, a severe form of malnutrition, could have been potentially significant if taken into consideration along with any arsenic in the house, as children and those with lower protein in the diet are more subject to arsenic poisoning. Of course, this does not explain why Martha did not succumb to such an illness, or why this occurred across households.

Robert Robinson, railway ganger and friend of Henry Needle, was next to the stand. Robinson and his wife had been

---

141 The earlier case stated 1885. He may have stayed with her on more than one occasion.
142 A severe form of malnutrition leading to wasting of the body including fat, muscle and body tissue.

neighbours who moved to Gippsland just before Henry's death. He revealed that Martha had suffered from typhoid fever, probably from living in the unhygienic slums of Richmond, which would help to explain reports of her headaches and delirium. This is highly contagious, with the vaccine against the microorganism that caused it not developed until 1911. Martha and her children and the guests of her house would have been at high risk of contracting the disease.

'The prisoner attended Henry Needle during his last illness, assisted by a neighbour towards the end. I saw Henry Needle the night before his death. He was a fairly strong man. The prisoner visited Gippsland twice in 1892.'

Gaunson asked, 'What was the prisoner's demeanour towards her husband?'

'She was invariably kind to her husband. Immediately after her husband's death, I understood she suffered from a slight attack of typhoid fever. When Elsie was ill there was nothing whatever suspicious in her conduct. May was always a sickly delicate child, and was thought at times to be at death's door. The prisoner spoke of the child as suffering from a bronchial infection.'

'Had you ever had a conversation with her about her late husband?'

'Yes. On one occasion when she was visiting us my wife and I were sympathising with her on the loss of her children, and said, "You would be glad if Harry were alive now." "No" she said, "If he were to walk in at that door I would not speak to him." The prisoner's demeanour was always kind to her children as a mother's should be, and the children were nicely kept.'

'Did she ever prevent you from seeing Harry Needle during his illness?'

'No, the prisoner never threw any obstacle in the way of my seeing Henry Needle during his illness. She seemed rather pleased to see me there, and there were no suspicious circumstances. I understand the medical attendant, Dr Singleton, was on friendly terms with the family.'

Detective Whitney was next asked to relate the circumstances surrounding the arrest of Martha. Gaunson tried his best to lead the jury and infuriate the witness. He exposed the failings of the police and the lack of proper processes taken in conducting the investigation.

'At what moment did Herman Juncken enter the house?'.... We are now on a serious matter of life and death...'

'He first entered the house, to the best of my belief, between 12 and 1 o'clock' said Whitney.

'For a sharp-witted detective like you, that is a very wide margin. Did you look at your watch?'

'I did when I went into the house myself.'

'Did you submit Herman Juncken to any search?'

'No.'

'Had you an opportunity of putting anything in the cup if you had chosen to?'

'I had not.'

'What was there to prevent you?'

'Herman Juncken had charge of the cup.'

'Had he had an opportunity?'

'Well, he had, I dare say.'

'Did you tell this unfortunate creature she need not answer any question which you might choose to put to her?'

'I did not. My caution was sufficient for that.'

'Was this an old gaol bird, or a person who had not been in any crime before?'

'She had never been in any crime to my knowledge.'

'Then that is your idea of a fair caution?' Gaunson paused.

'Did you suspect at the time she went towards the shelf that she intended to take her life with chlorodyne?'

'I did not know what the bottle contained at the time, but I took every precaution that she should not take her life by any means.'

'Do you remember swearing, on the occasion when I applied for bail, that she had tried to take her life on that occasion?'

'I don't remember ever swearing that. I remember distinctly swearing that in my opinion she would, if admitted to bail, commit suicide.'

'Did you by sweeping or washing the floors, or in any way, attempt to find remains of the vomit of Louis Juncken?'

'The floors were perfectly clean. In fact, it was as clean a house as ever I was in.'

Gaunson then tried to arouse sympathy for his client. 'Do you know as a matter of fact that Otto Juncken has been prevented from speaking to her?'

Judge Hodges advised Whitney, 'Unless you know of your own knowledge, don't answer.'

'I know Otto Juncken has been allowed to speak to her,' said Whitney.

'Do you know of your own knowledge that he has been refused? Did you refuse him yourself?'

'I have refused him a dozen times,' Whitney admitted.

Judge Hodges commented, 'It is the ordinary course.'

Gaunson replied, 'I don't know if it is the ordinary course, but to me it seems an illegal course. The accused is not a convicted person. However, we need not discuss that now, for I just propose to mention it to the jury.'

'You say you took certain old bottles or jars out of the dresser cupboard?' Gaunson asked.

'No, I took them out of the cupboard by the fireplace, and the corks out of a drawer in the dresser.'

'Then Otto Juncken is not correct when he says you took them out of the bottom part of the dresser?'

'Otto Juncken was not present. I searched all parts of the dresser, and it was not possible for smeared bread and butter to have been either there or in the cupboard without my seeing it. I also searched in the cupboard under the stairs.'

'Did you search with a keen anxiety to preserve this woman from an unfounded charge?'

'I did...We had a candle when searching under the stairs.'

'Had you a search warrant or any authority permitting you to interfere with the accused's property in any way?'

'No.'

'Did you oppose the application I made for bail?'

'I did. It was my firm belief that if admitted to bail, the prisoner would commit suicide. It is my opinion that there are more cases of suicide amongst persons of sound mind than amongst those of unsound mind.'

'Then suicide is a sign of sanity?'

There were some giggles from the audience.

Judge Hodges became frustrated, 'What has this to do with the case? Is this important?'

In reply, Gaunson asked Whitney, 'Is that what you say?'

'I have heard of more people of sound mind committing suicide than lunatics.'

'So that you believe that self-destruction is rather an evidence of soundness of mind than otherwise? For what it is worth, is that your opinion?'

'No, it is not.'

'What did the prisoner say when you served her with a notice that there was to be an exhumation of her husband's body?'

'She asked me if I would like the names of a few more of her friends that had died with a view to taking them up. I said "No, thank you, I have quite enough at present."'

'The prisoner said that in a sober, serious sort of way?'

'Yes.'

Dr Hodgson and Dr Payne were the next witnesses in the box. After Dr Payne conveyed his evidence, Martha Needle rose from her chair, and, advancing to the front of the dock, said 'May I speak your Honour?'

Judge Hodges replied, 'You may, but it would be better to consult your legal advisor.'

Gaunson went over to the witness box, and had a conversation with Martha, returning back to the witness.

'There is one question I would like to ask Dr Payne, your Honour.'

'Certainly,' replied Hodges.

'Was it at your suggestion or that of the prisoner that Dr Burton was called in?'

'I can't say positively, but I believe I suggested it.'

'If the prisoner says that it was her desire and suggestion, and that you delayed three or four days, and that she was dissatisfied, would you swear that was false?'

'I will swear it is false I delayed for three or four days.'

'Then you cannot say as to the rest of the question. This is very important.'

'I cannot say at this length of time whether it was I or the prisoner who suggested it, but to the best of my belief it was I.

'If she says she was the first to suggest it, will you contradict her?'

'I won't contradict her. I cannot tell whether it was the prisoner or myself who first suggested extra medical skill.' At the conclusion of this statement, the witness was asked to return to the dock.

Finlayson rose. 'That is all of the evidence I propose to present for the prosecution. There are further witnesses that could be called, but I will not, unless Mr Gaunson desires them to be.'

Gaunson replied, 'I wish to call Mrs Georgina Lillis, followed by Mrs Eliza Martin.' Mrs Lillis came to the witness box and repeated her evidence from the previous trial.

'Did Mrs Needle show any ill-will towards Louis Juncken?' asked Gaunson.

'I saw nothing to show that Mrs Needle had any ill-will against Louis.'

'What did you do during those fits?'

'I did nothing but sit beside her.'

Georgina Lillis was asked to sit down and then Eliza Martin was called to the witness box. Eliza told again of her early life in South Australia, how Martha was beaten with a stick and rope by her mother when she was young and how she claimed that her mother was not her real mother. Eliza told the story that she had told at the police court, of one instance when Martha was not in her usual state, in greater detail.

'One bitterly cold night last winter, about 12 o'clock, I was in bed, and she came to my house without her jacket, her hat on one side of her head, and looking very wild. She knocked very hard at the door and asked me to let her in as a man had followed her all the way from her place. But she sat on the step instead of coming in. There was a man outside.'

'Who was that man?' asked Gaunson.

'The man outside was Otto Juncken. After a lot of persuasion, I got her inside the house. Otto remained outside at the gate. She would not let him in. She did not appear to know him. I said to her "That is Otto," and she replied, "It is not Otto! That man has followed me all the way down from my place."'

'She kept talking about her children, wishing that they were not dead and looking for them in the bed. I persuaded her to come into the kitchen, when she said she was going to the cemetery to see the children's graves. I got her to sit down and wait for a cup of tea, and to coax her, I said I would go with her to the cemetery. She sat down on a chair, and went into a fit which lasted about three quarters of an hour. Otto came inside, and had to hold her to prevent her from falling. It must have been past 1 o'clock when they went away, and then she was not properly conscious. Otto had to put his arm around her to support her.'

Gaunson asked Eliza more about Martha's upbringing in Adelaide.

'Mrs Foran was unkind to the accused and she would beat her severely with a stick. Daniel Foran was a blackguard.[143] The accused home was peculiarly wretched. The accused said to me "My mother died when I was born and Mrs Foran was only taking care of me." I was inclined to believe that because Mrs Foran was kinder to the other children than she was to the accused. Only a few months since, she said she was entitled to some property, that her father had died in England, leaving her, his only child, some hundreds of pounds. I thought it strange and I hoped it was true, but I did not know whether to believe her or not.'

'Have you heard of any attempts to kill her mother?'

'I never heard at Adelaide that any attempt had been made to poison Mrs Foran at any time. The accused gets awfully

---

143 A dishonourable man.

excited sometimes and she says it is caused by pains in her head. She said "Oh, these pains in my head will either kill me or drive me mad." She seemed to be serious when she said that. 'You were fond of her?'

Eliza paused, holding back tears, 'Yes.'

'And you believed her to be a good woman?'

'I believe her to be a good woman now.' Eliza Martin was asked to stand down from the witness box. The day concluded with Gaunson indicating that he did not wish to call any more witnesses.

It was then time for the barristers to address the jury. Finlayson argued that his opening statement had been borne out by the evidence presented. Gaunson needed more time to present to the jury. He asked that the court be adjourned until the following morning so that he could refer to his shorthand notes of the evidence.

*

The following morning, Gaunson addressed the jury on behalf of Martha in what was described by the press as a powerful speech. He first remarked on the painful and dramatic character of the case.

'I would like to call attention to what I consider the extraordinary, ill-advised, improper and illegal reports and comments which have appeared in various newspapers in regard to Mrs Needle and her alleged crimes.'

'I contend that the evidence has utterly failed to suggest any motive for the crimes, or to prove that the prisoner had administered arsenic to Louis Juncken, Herman Juncken, her husband, and her children. There has been gross carelessness shown in the post-mortem examination and the analyses.'

'It is all nonsense to suppose that the accused would be in a conscious state if she did murder her children. There was ample evidence presented of long periods of unconsciousness on the part of the accused. I do not want you, the jury, to understand that I think that the accused has done any of the acts with which she is charged. I am simply putting this to you so that if any of you might have thought she had committed the acts, you might still take into consideration the question of whether she was responsible or not for her actions.'

After three and a half hours addressing the jury, Mr Justice Hodges summed up the case. He urged the men of the jury, 'You have to decide the case, not on what you may have heard outside or from counsel in court, or from what you have read in the newspapers, but on the evidence which has come before you in the course of the case. The allegation here is that the accused murdered Louis Juncken, and it is said on behalf of the Crown that his death was compassed[144] by the administration of arsenic or arsenious acid.'

'You have to be satisfied beyond reasonable doubt that Louis Juncken died from arsenic or arsenious acid, and that the prisoner intentionally administered that poison. If you are satisfied beyond reasonable doubt of those two facts, the prisoner is guilty of the offence with which she is charged. If your mind is left in a state of reasonable doubt, then the prisoner is entitled to the benefit of that doubt, and the verdict will be one of not guilty.'

'You will understand you are trying the prisoner for the murder of Louis Juncken – not for the murder of Henry Needle, or for the attempted murder of Herman Juncken. The

---

144 Perhaps a religious inference. King James Bible Psalm 116:3 states 'The sorrows of death compassed me, and the pains of hell gat hold upon me: I found trouble and sorrow.'

facts relating to those persons are brought before you for the purpose of enabling you to say whether or not Louis Juncken died from poison, and whether that poison got accidentally or intentionally into his body.'

'It is not necessary for me to go further back in the history of the case than the early part of 1892, when the prisoner went to keep house for the Junckens at Bridge Road, Richmond. In the April of that year Otto and Louis Juncken appear to have gone away for a couple of days' holiday, and when Otto returned he found awaiting him a letter from the prisoner – a letter which I will not read, but which, no doubt, is a piteous, pitiable letter – a letter of despair, showing it was her intention to commit suicide, and that at that time she entertained for Otto Juncken feelings which indicated that he would not have been unacceptable to her as a husband. The letter indicated that she regarded him as her closest friend, and she left him certain small memoriums, suggesting how she would like her property distributed, and pointing out where, if she died, she would like to be buried. That letter may have been a genuine expression of her state of mind and feeling or it may not. It has been suggested that it was put together for the purpose of stirring emotions in the breast of Otto Juncken, but it is an evidence that she did attempt to carry out on her body what that letter suggested. Otto that same evening, however, obtained a promise that she would not carry out her threat of committing suicide.'

'You will easily understand, although there might have been no previous love passages between prisoner and Otto Juncken, that in the case of a woman who is not altogether without attractions – a woman weak and in a bad state of health – such a letter would draw forth his sympathy and kindly feeling, and you can well understand how these feelings might give rise to the warm affection which resulted in the engagement between Otto and the prisoner. At that time all his family seemed to agree to the engagement, and according to the evidence it was the prisoner who suggested that the marriage should be postponed for some time on account of her ill health.'

'In November of that year, 1892, all appearing to be going on harmoniously, the prisoner visited South Australia for about five weeks. On her return, the manner of Louis appeared to undergo change, and the prisoner complained of that change. That is so, if you believe the evidence of Otto. It is all a question of whom you believe and whom you do not believe; and you will have to say whether you believe the evidence of Otto in the painful position in which he is placed. You have to say whether while the witness Otto Juncken was standing in the box giving evidence on oath, evidence which might affect the fate of the woman he loved – you have to say whether under those circumstances he has, not only according to his own evidence but according to all the evidence, has conducted himself as to inspire you with absolute confidence in everything he said. As a man he appears to have controlled not only the warmth of his feelings but controlled his thoughts in a manner worthy of the biggest praise – a character manly, noble, and generous to a degree.'

'If you believe Otto, then undoubtedly at that time there occurred differences between Louis and the accused. While that difference existed, there appears to have been a communication between Otto and his mother with a view of bringing on the marriage in May, 1893, and the mother opposed the marriage on the ground of the prisoner's ill health. The prisoner appears to have resented this, and to have written a violent letter, which caused Mrs Juncken to object to the marriage, not only on the ground of the prisoner's ill health but also on the ground of her ill-temper. That was in May or June or soon after.'

'In a case of murder, it is not incumbent on the prosecution to prove the motive, but it is required to see whether there is a possible or provable and sufficient motive for the crime. The prisoner first discovers the coldness arising between Louis and herself, and then since finds the mother interfering to put off the marriage. Did she in her mind at that time connect, or suppose, or believe, that this was a family matter, and that Louis and the mother were working together to prevent her marriage? If she did and if she were a person who placed little value on human life, it might furnish her with some motive to induce her to do the act with which she is charged. I only mention that as a slight suggestion of a motive which the prisoner may have had.'

'Whilst the condition of affairs existed, Louis, on the 18$^{th}$ August 1893, was taken very ill. You will find at that time the first symptom was vomiting. Now, it is important for you to note what the start is, how the illness commenced, and what the symptoms are; and you will note that before ever a doctor is seen – before ever any medicine is taken or anything which came from any chemist – the symptom is vomiting. The Crown suggests that arsenic caused it. I don't know what is suggested on behalf of the prisoner before this that it is not proved it was arsenic, or that it is possible the putrefactive pus coming from the jaw caused the sickness. How the pus started from the jaw, we don't know, assuming it was there.'

'Louis went to Dr MacColl, who found what he called putrefactive pus being discharged from underneath the jaw, and considering that the man had 'Riggs' disease,' treated him accordingly. Louis was ill for about 10 days, and then he recovered. Apart from the affectation to the jaw, we are told that he appeared to be a sound and healthy man. Then, on the 25$^{th}$ April, the following year, he is taken ill again. And again before even he sees a doctor – before any medicine is applied – he is vomiting. Again, gentleman, what caused the vomiting?'

'You will remember that Dr Neild's opinion is that the pus was not the pus of Riggs' disease of the jaw, but that the administration of arsenic would produce the pus. However, Dr MacColl was undoubtedly strongly of the opinion that the deceased had Riggs' disease, and that possibly some of the pus was getting down into the stomach and causing irritation and vomiting. The view of the Crown is that it was nothing of the kind, but that it was arsenic. On the 26th April, the day after, he again went to see Dr MacColl, who then suggested that he was a little feverish and might have typhoid. Then a Mrs Emma Jones came over to Melbourne, and it is suggested that from this time Louis improved; and undoubtedly he did improve.'

'Mrs Jones left about the 8$^{th}$ May, and on the 9$^{th}$, Louis was up out of bed. And now we come to the part on which the Crown lays great stress. They say that all of the symptoms were not inconsistent with poisoning with arsenious acid; and then they say that on the evening of the 10$^{th}$ May, just as this improvement was taking place, and as they fancied, the patient was out of danger, the prisoner purchased a box containing arsenious acid in the form of 'Rough on Rats.' On the 11$^{th}$, the day following, Louis was worse again, and it is suggested that if Louis had arsenic before he was gradually recovering from the effects of it, and that on the 10$^{th}$ more was purchased. On the 11$^{th}$ Louis is very bad. It is said that the prisoner herself suggested another doctor. Of course, if that be so it is in her favour, or it might be suggested that she was satisfied as to her success. The deceased got worse, and on the 16^th he died.'

'Now we come to what took place a short time afterwards. Louis was buried at Lyndoch, but in consequence of something that took place suspicions were aroused, and the body was exhumed and portions of it analysed. It has been said that you have nothing to do with judging Mr Blackett's honesty. I think you have everything to do with his honesty. If he be not an honest man, we cannot place much reliance on what he says. But you have two things to be satisfied about in regard to Mr Blackett – his honesty and his capacity. You have two things to be satisfied of in regard to Dr Neild – his honesty and his capacity.

'The body of Louis was exhumed, and Dr Neild took the stomach and intestines, one lung, and the heart, and sent them on to Mr Blackett. Every precaution was taken in regard to the cleansing of the vessels in which those portions of the body were contained. The stomach was analysed, and while this, as I understand, is how Mr Blackett conducted the analysis, he has – and I understand it is the usual thing to do – he has not analysed the whole of the stomach and intestines, nor has he taken a third of the stomach and intestines from one place. He has cut portions from different parts so as to get 1 oz, which might fairly represent the whole stomach, and be a fair average of the whole. I don't assume, and Mr Blackett does not assume, that the arsenic was equally distributed throughout the whole of the stomach and intestines, but that he considers that what he has taken is a fair sample of the whole stomach. In the portions that he took he found not quite a grain of arsenious acid, and assuming that these portions are a fair sample of the whole, Mr Blackett says there were about 3.3 grains of arsenic in the whole body. If that was the amount, it was abundant to cause death. Mr Blackett absolutely found arsenious acid in the body and according to modern medical opinion arsenic is no part of the human body. The deceased, so far as we know, had taken no medicine in which there was arsenic. It is said this arsenic might have come from bismuth, which sometimes has arsenious acid in it, but Mr Blackett had sent to him some of the bismuth taken out of the bottles from which the bismuth administered to the deceased was taken, and he said that in that bismuth there is no arsenic. He tells you that in modern times, drugs have become purer in consequence of various acts of Parliament. So the prosecution says, "here is arsenious acid found in the body of Louis Juncken, here is arsenious acid found in the possession of the prisoner." The prisoner attended to him, and, they say, it is reasonable to suppose she administered the arsenic to him. There was no other hand, they say, from which he could have received it. Then Dr Neild was examined, and he says:

"The symptoms I saw were consistent with death from arsenious acid; and if arsenious acid were found in the stomach and intestines, I am of the opinion that arsenious acid was the cause of death."

'You will see that Dr Neild does not say that the symptoms he saw would be consistent with death from no other cause; and I suppose it would hardly be possible to find a case where symptoms discovered in a body some time after burial might not be consistent with death from several causes. But Dr Neild says "I see in the body appearances consistent with death from arsenious acid. I find arsenious acid there, and therefore I infer that death arose from arsenious acid." Now, gentleman, you have to be satisfied that the prisoner administered the arsenic, and administered it intentionally. One might suppose that where Rough on Rats was in the place and the greatest care was not used in cleaning the spoon or article used to apply it that it might innocently get into the stomach of some person in the house. But the prosecution says that in this case the arsenic was administered intentionally and showed that in all the cases in which arsenious acid was found in the bodies and in the case of Herman Juncken the symptoms were the same.'

'In the body of Henry Needle, who died in October 1889, there were 1.4 grains of arsenic acid found, and in his case there was persistent vomiting. The case as regard to Elsie Needle is somewhat weaker, for only an infinitesimal portion of arsenic was found, and the evidence is not so clear as to the vomiting. In the body of May Needle 2 grains of arsenic were found, and there again vomiting was the chief symptom. Dr Payne, who attended May, says that the case attracted his attention, and now, hearing that arsenic was found in the body, he has no hesitation in saying that death was caused by arsenical poisoning. On behalf of the prisoner it is said that, in the case of May, another medical expert was called in at her instigation. Dr Payne says that he does not remember that, but it might be thought that the doctor would have remembered if the suggestion had been made by the prisoner.'

'Now we come to what possibly in this case bears mostly hardly against the prisoner. It is very extraordinary in its circumstances and its surroundings. The prisoner hears, and perhaps not unnaturally, the proposal that she should separate from Otto for a time and that the marriage should be further postponed, but according to the evidence she appears to have made up her mind about it, and to have taken initiative steps to getting a housekeeper's place. Herman Juncken up to that time had been friendly as one of the family who was not against her. On the 3$^{rd}$ of June, the day after he arrived from South

Australia with Otto, Herman had the interview with the prisoner in reference to her relations with his mother. Herman says the prisoner then went into what he imagined to be a sham faint. It may have been a sham faint, or it may not, and the news as to the separation was unpleasant to the prisoner.'

'Up to that time, although he had had his meals in the house, Herman had had no ill health or symptoms of ill health. The morning afterwards he was seized with vomiting immediately after his breakfast of tea and fried eggs, the latter of which his brother Otto had cooked. That breakfast was served by the prisoner. He went to his friends, the Smiths, and stayed there until the 8th, on the night of the 6th the vomiting had ceased, and there was no vomiting on the 7th. On the 8th he called at Mrs Needle's and had some tea and bread and butter, and he immediately became ill and commenced vomiting. He then went to Smith's and saw Dr Boyd, who seems to have had some suspicion, and asked that the vomit should be kept. This was done. And it is important to remember that the vomit kept was the second, and that it happened before he had taken any medicine at all, or anything, in any shape or form, after the tea and bread and butter.'

'In that vomit Mr Blackett subsequently found strong traces of arsenic. It is suggested that the vessel in which the vomit was kept was not clean. Of course, that is possible, but if the arsenic was already in the vessel it is very curious what caused the vomiting. No other cause but arsenic has been attributed or suggested. The fried eggs are suggested as the cause on the first occasion, but the second he had only had tea and bread and butter. Of course, suspicion was thoroughly aroused, and then, at the suggestion of the detectives, Herman went to Mrs Needle's house at lunch time on the 15th June. The only cup or vessel in which arsenic was found was in the cup of tea prepared for Herman by the prisoner and in that were found 10.5 grains of arsenic. Now, it is said that proper precautions were not taken to wash out the jars in which the detectives placed the food they seized. It is very singular if by some chance the vessel into which the cup of tea was put was the only vessel which had arsenic in it.'

'It is difficult to understand how such a set of circumstances could weave themselves around this unfortunate woman.'

'The jars were washed out and clean as they could be made. If Herman or the police did not put arsenic in the cup, how did it get there? You are not trying the prisoner for this case, which is only used for the purpose of showing the effects of arsenical poisoning by arsenious acid, and in order to show that it must have been infinitesimal. As to the observations about bismuth and calomel, Mr Blackett found neither of these, and in ordinary doses calomel does not produce disastrous results. You have not to deal with possibilities but more with probabilities; and you have to say whether, having viewed all those facts, that Louis Juncken – don't forget that it is for his death the prisoner is being tried – died in consequence of arsenious acid, and that it got into his body through the hands of the prisoner, and that she intended to kill him.'

'There is one defence put up on behalf of the prisoner, and that is that it might have been done when she was of unsound mind. You are told there are differences between doctors and lawyers as to what insanity is. I don't know that there is in the proper sense of the term a difference between one and the other, bar in the law and justice, which cannot wait while philosophers, physicians, and scientists settle metaphysical problems. It has been compelled to arrive at a definition of the state of mind which would absolve a man from criminal responsibility. Justice must be swift and sure; and the definition is this – if you should arrive at the conclusion – on what evidence I really do not know – that the prisoner did administer this arsenious acid, but she did not know the nature and quality of the act she was committing – that she did not know that what she was doing was taking life, or that taking life was wrong – then you will find her not guilty on the ground of insanity. I do not know where you will get evidence on which you would arrive at the conclusion that when she administered this poison, if she did administer it, she was in that frame of mind; but if you can see any ground on which you can arrive at such a conclusion, of course you are entitled to arrive at it. I don't know of any evidence to suggest such a conclusion.'

'It is right on behalf of the prisoner that I should conclude what I have to say with the observation that no witness called has suggested that she was not uniformly kind to her husband and children, or that she ever had a hostile or unkindly feeling towards them. The only expression against her was that she was said to have threatened not to speak to her husband if he walked in at the door. On the other hand, whatever may have been the feelings she outwardly showed, there are the bodies – there are the records of persistent vomiting – there is the motive – whether it was that she did not want to speak to her husband any more or because she thought the children an encumbrance – whatever it was, there is the arsenic and there are the symptoms. If you have any reasonable doubt in your minds, she is entitled to the benefit of that doubt. Reasonable doubt does not mean possibilities such as that Mr Blackett found no arsenic at all, that they were the wrong bodies, that the witnesses are all lying, and such possibilities as that. You have to remember that a human life is at stake, and have to feel a reasonable certainty in your convictions.'

*

At the conclusion of Justice Hodges's summing up, the jury went to lunch and then met to consider their verdict. Just forty five minutes after the commencement of their meeting, the jury returned to the court. The spokesman for the jury was called, he rose, and swiftly pronounced the verdict of 'Guilty.' Martha, seated beside two female wardens from the prison, gasped upon hearing the verdict, but showed no other emotion.

The Judge's associate, Mr Pearson, said, 'Martha Needle, have you anything to say why sentence of death should not be passed on you?'

Martha responded quietly, 'I am not guilty.' No one could hear her response. She spoke louder, 'It is undeserved. I am not guilty.' Perhaps her denial was a defence mechanism towards a truth she could now not contemplate.

Justice Hodges replied, 'It is not my intention to keep you one moment in suspense. If conscience is not already doing its work, nothing that I can say will have any effect. It is my duty only to pronounce the sentence of the Court.'

Judge Hodges then passed the penalty of the death sentence.

Upon the conclusion of the case, all in the court room rose and filtered out. Martha remained with her two attendants, and according to a newspaper report was 'the least disturbed of them all.' After the crowd had left, Martha walked from the dock with the guards, without any assistance, in order to go back to her gaol cell.

# 8

# Final Pleas, Salvation and Redemption

The sentencing of Martha Needle renewed public interest in The Richmond Poisoning Case and re-emergence of newspapers stories throughout Australia and New Zealand. The press emphasised the role of the evidence used in the case with respect to the entire Needle family, evidence which today would be disallowed as it did not directly relate to the crimes for which Martha Needle was tried. *The Argus* praised this fact. In the views of the press and the general public, Martha had been justly tried and found guilty of the murder of her entire family along with that of Louis Juncken.[145]

This public belief in Martha being responsible for a range of crimes for which she was not tried for was exemplified in a letter to the editor of *The Argus* criticising the practice of cremation.[146] Cremation was a topic for public debate during this period, and the practice would soon be introduced throughout Australia. The author of the letter suggested that the unreliability of the various doctors' diagnoses was an important factor to consider in the cremation debate. The

---

145  The Argus 6th October 1894
146  The Argus, 2nd October 1894.

question of whether arsenic could be found in cremated remains was of keen interest to scientists reporting in the Indian Medical Gazette of 1941, who found that it was, in fact, still possible to detect arsenic following cremation.[147]

Mrs Ada Owen and Otto supported Martha to the end. Mrs Owen, a deeply religious woman, was keen for Martha to find solace in religion, urging her to seek consolation in Jesus and thereby achieve salvation. She kept up an avid correspondence with Martha during her final days.

*Tooronga Road*
*Auburn*
*Oct 5<sup>th</sup> 1894*

*Dear Mrs Needle*

*I could not tell you on Tuesday as I wanted to what a precious friend you would find in Jesus, but I want to tell you now that if you only trust him he will never leave you or forsake you, I do hope that before this you will have realised his love to you; it passes knowledge the great love he has shown to us, and if we will only believe in him he will help us whatever trouble or trial we may have. Even though we may walk through the valley of the shadow of death he has promised to be with us, and we need not fear whatever may happen having him we have all, we may cast for every care over on him for he careth for us.*

*I am still praying that you may have faith to believe in him, and I know if you will do so he will help you because his word is sure, nothing in my hand I bring simply to thy*

---

147  Chakravarti, S.N., Faruqi, M.Z & Ganguly, K. R. (1941). Detection of Arsenic in Burnt Human Bones and Ashes, *Indian Medical Gazette*, December 1941.

*cross I cling. The Lord bless thee and keep thee, the Lord make his face shine upon thee, and lift up his countenance upon thee and give thee peace*

*I remain your sincere friend.*
*Ada Owen*

Ada also added the words from a hymn written by Charlotte Elliot, entitled 'Just as I Am,' which was about turning from sin and finding salvation.

*Just as I am – thy love unknown,*

*Has broken every barrier down Now to be thine, yea thine alone Oh, Lamb of God I come!*

After the death sentence was passed down, it was challenged by progressive Solicitor Marshall Lyle, who had represented Frederick Bailey Deeming ('The Demon'), a murderer also replicated in the Chamber of Horrors at Kreitmayer's Waxworks Exhibition. He had represented Deeming with Alfred Deakin, barrister, who would become an Australian Prime Minister. Deeming's case was heard two years' prior, when his defence of insanity for violently murdering his second wife (having previously murdered his first wife and children in England) was unsuccessful and he was eventually hanged. In 1892, Irishman Lyle had written to the Governor and members of the Executive Council regarding the Deeming case,[148] and

---

148  See: http://www.prov.vic.gov.au/online-exhibitions/deeming/documents/
    vprs264-p0-u21-lyleletter2a.htm and http://www.prov.vic.gov.au/online-

he did the same for Martha Needle. Lyle believed that Martha should be reprieved due to her mental state, and first wrote to Arthur Akehurst at the Crown Law Department regarding her mental state and requested an examination of Martha by competent medical professionals. Lyle was interested in criminal anthropology, medico-legal science and studies of mental disorder and strongly held the view that medical science should take precedence over popular understandings of insanity and traditional legal traditions.[149]

*The Camperdown Chronicle* reported on the 9th October that:

*In reply, Mr A P Akehurst sent the following letter to Mr Lyle:-*

*Sir, I received your second letter this morning, and submitted it to the hon. The Premier.*

*He desires me to point out that you have not yet disclosed the facts you previously alluded to; and he considers the evidence adduced at the trial does not furnish any ground for a suggestion of insanity, no evidence whatever having been called to support such a theory.*

*If you desire your application to be further considered, it is necessary for you to submit further particulars of the information which you said had reached you on the subject.*

*AN EXTRAORDINARY LETTER*

*Mr Lyle, in reply to this communication, has forwarded the following letter to Mr Akehurst, which speaks for itself:-*

exhibitions/deeming/documents/vprs264-p0-u21-LyleLetter3.htm
149  Evans, C. 'Responsibility and criminal law in the late-nineteenth-century British Empire.' The Howard League for Penal Reform, ECAN Bulletin, Issue 23, June 2014.

*Sir, I beg to acknowledge the receipt of yours of the 8th instant. Your first letter was based on an untrue statement of facts. Your second shows a desire to avoid the whole matter, You do not dispute my statement that the reason you have for not carrying out your duty was false in fact, and showed that no intelligent inquiry had been made. But you suggest two other excuses for not doing so. In reply to my request that you should ascertain facts as to the sanity or insanity of the prisoner, you reply now that you will not do so unless I supply you with facts as to the sanity or insanity of the prisoner. There can be no facts of any such character independent of careful personal examination. What I may have heard is as worthless as anything you may have heard. If the Premier intended something more sensible be written, as a further excuse, it certainly has not been done. The Premier takes it upon himself to assassinate by his agent, relying upon a bland assumption that he is competent to express an opinion as to mental disease.*

*We believe that there can be no successful warfare against crime and criminals until the principle can be recognised that the scientific examination of the dangerous members of society is the duty of the State, assisted by intelligent officials. This principle is now refused even a slight recognition, but demanded by rapidly progressing science and increasing desire of the public for greater security against criminals must yet make its way into a Victorian politician-managed Department of Justice.*

*Mr Lyle now intends forwarding a petition to his Excellency the Governor, praying for a commutation of the death penalty.*

*The Weekly Times, 13th October 1894*

A petition was then made to the Governor of Victoria and the Executive Council of government on the Needle case by Marshall Lyle who was the Australian representative for the Howard Association for Penal Reform in Australia (a network based in the UK which still exists as the Howard League for Penal Reform) and presented on the 16th October 1894. Not only an advocate for medico-legal advances, Lyle was a strong advocate against capital punishment. The new Premier of Victoria, Solicitor (and later Sir) George Turner, in office for less than one month, was reluctant to let politics get in the way of the legal process. He responded to the Howard Association letter by saying that there were no new facts bearing on the case, and that the law should take its course.[150] The warrant authorising the execution had already been signed and the date of execution was set for Monday, 22nd October 1894. Meanwhile, it was reported in *The Weekly Times* that Martha's lawyer David Gaunson had given up on the case, as he was of the understanding that Martha wished to die and that 'he was of the opinion that it would be useless to take any further action in the case.'[151] On the 17th October, Martha had written out her will with the assistance of Mr Gaunson, leaving all that she had, a life insurance policy of £50, to Otto.

When Martha was told of the decision of the Executive Council by the Governor of the Gaol, she said 'Thank you, Sir' in a calm demeanour which reportedly 'did not betray the slightest agitation of mind,'[152] and then Martha turned to her attendants to ask mundane questions. In her last letter to Mrs Owen, Martha thought about comforting her friend beyond her own death.

---

150  The Argus, 17th October 1894
151  The Weekly Times, 13th October 1894
152  The Argus, 10th October 1894

*Martha Needle, H.M. Gaol Melbourne,*
*October 16th 1894*
*My kind and dear friend,*

*You must not think me forgetful for not thanking you today for all you have done for me during the laste fore long and uneasy months for I have not forgot aney one's kindness to me now or at aney time. Dear friend I hope you all will try not to grive too much for me hard as I know that will be for you all. You asked me to day if you could do aney thing for me the oney thing you can do is to be as good a friend to Otto as you have been to me for years. Dear boy he deserves evry loving kindness for his manleyis[153] to me. I know dear friend I must bide you a last and found good by from your ernes Loving friend*

*Martha Needle*

On the back of this letter, Martha writes a verse from a famous hymn written in 1824 by a Scotsman, Henry Lyte, a pastor and writer of hymns who had been orphaned as a child:

*Jesus I My Cross have taken*[154]

*Jesus, I my cross have taken,*
*All to leave and follow Thee.*
*Destitute, despised, forsaken,*
*Thou from hence my all shall be.*
*Perish every fond ambition,*

---

153  Manliness.
154  This verse is still popular. The full verse can be found at: http://hymnbook.igracemusic.com/hymns/jesus-i-my-cross-have-taken and a modern version can be heard at: https://www.youtube.com/watch?v=NhIo2o3WLnA

*All I've sought or hoped or known.*
*Yet how rich is my condition!*
*God and heaven are still my own.*

*From Martha with Love to dear Ada*

In her prison bible, the New Testament, on the page of the 'First Epistle General of John,' Martha underlined some passages, suggesting that she had indeed found comfort in Jesus, as her friend had hoped for:

*But if we walk in the light as he is in the light, we have fellowship one with another, and <u>the blood of Jesus Christ his Son cleanseth us from all sin</u>.*

*If we say that we have no sin, we deceive ourselves, and the truth is not in us.*

<u>*If we confess our sins, he is faithful and just to cleanse us our sins, and to cleanse us from all unrighteousness*</u>.

Martha's underlining of 'confessing our sins' may have been some sort of confession in itself. On the same page, Martha wrote: 'Dear Ada, God be with you all, till we meet again, M Needle.' On another page, Martha left another message behind:

*The proof that I am weak is*
*this When left without*
*support I fall The strength*
*in which I stand is his Who*
*to his saints is all in all*[155]

---

155  State Library of Victoria, Martha Needle papers, MSS 8296

The issue of Martha confessing to her crimes was a great consternation for Church of England Chaplain, Reverend Henry Scott of the Old Melbourne Gaol. It was now his job to see that he 'saved her soul' by ensuring that she repented of her sins. It had been his job as chaplain to attend to Martha in the weeks leading up to her death. Just the night before her hanging, Martha had an altercation with Reverend Scott. The Reverend was concerned to get an oral confession from Martha, on behalf of one or more jurors who were concerned about the sentence they had passed. The Reverend saw Otto as an 'obstacle' to such a confession, as Otto had led Martha to trust that he believed her innocent. The Reverend wished Otto to tell Martha that he believed she had committed the crimes with full knowledge of her actions and took the liberty of telling Martha that Otto believed she had committed her crimes with full knowledge and intent. This deeply angered Martha, but she refused to believe the Reverend and called him a liar.[156]

The Reverend was extremely frustrated with Martha, and he had a very different experience with 'babyfarmer' Frances Knorr earlier in 1894: Knorr had prayed with and sung hymns with him before her death. Knorr's was an eventful hanging, as the usual hangman had died by suicide two days before the event —his wife had threatened to leave him if he carried through the act.[157] The Reverend was able to assure Knorr of the 'forgiveness and mercy of God' and 'accepted her true repentance for all her sins.'[158]

*

---

156 The Argus, 22nd October 1894
157 Display, Old Melbourne Gaol.
158 Display, Old Melbourne Gaol.

On the night before the execution, aroused by the turmoil and inner conflict from her altercation with the Reverend, Martha found it difficult to sleep, and she woke up at 4 am and wrote a letter to Otto.

> *Melbourne Gaol,*
> *Monday, 4 o'clock [am]*

*My darling – As you wished me to write, I will do so, but truly I do not know what to say to you on this, my last morning on earth. In a few hours I shall be free from all sorrow, but you, dear Otto, must live on for a time. It may be a very long time or it may not, but whichever way God wishes it will be. But never mind, try to bear up under the very sad blow. Rest assured we shall meet again where there is no parting. Your good father, also poor Louis, and my dear little ones will welcome you. You know dear Elsie and May loved you on earth. They will do so in heaven. Think how they will all welcome you to our happy home on high. I must ask you not to think unkindly of me for saying what I did last night to Mr. Scott. I think it right that you should know what that man did say about you, but I want you to thoroughly understand that I did not believe that you ever did say so to him, and I told him so. You must not think what he said about me upset me, for it did not; only it annoyed me to think that such a man would tell an untruth. True, he may think he was doing right. We must hope he did think so. Now, you will want to know what sort of a night I have had. Fairly good. You and all my dear ones have been in my thoughts and prayers. Dear Otto, please read the 139th psalm from the 7th to the 13th verse. As I have asked God to forgive me anything that I have done to displease Him, and trust to His forgiveness, so do*

*I forgive all that have ever done me any sort of unkindness. For I know that they are very sorry now for me, be the wrong little or big. Give my everlasting love to all inquiring friends. I must now say goodbye to you for a time. When you receive this you can think of me as being in a happy home with my loved ones, waiting and watching for you. I know, dear Otto, that you will get ready for that happy meeting with us all. With love and sympathy – From your loving Martha.*[159]

Another hymn was written on the back of the official gaol letter paper, and dated Monday morning, 6 o'clock. This was a slight adaptation of a scripture 'Farewell Hymn'[160] composed by Henry Bishop:

*Farewell, faithful ones, I must bid adieu
To all the joys and pleasures I have tasted with you.
We labor together, united in heart.
But now I must leave you, and soon we must part.*

*My labours are over and I must be gone,
But I leave you, not friendless, to struggle alone,*

*Be watchful and prayerful, and Jesus will stay.
Cleave close to your Saviour; let Him lead the way.*

*Farewell, dear one, sad time now with you,
My heart sinks within me at bidding you adieu
One step back or forward would settle me doom
'Mid the glories of Heaven or return, it is gloom.*

---

159  From: The *Weekly Times*
160  Scripture Acts 18:21. See: https://hymnary.org/tune/
farewell_faithful_friends_we_must_bishop

*Farewell, my dear one, I now go away,*
*No more to meet you till the great Judgment Day.*
*Though absent in body I'm with you in prayer.*
*And we'll meet in Heaven. There's no parting there.*

Martha enclosed another note for Otto, written on half a sheet of gaol notepaper which read as follows:

*My Last Prayer*

*'This will be my last prayer in thought:-*

*Almighty God, to whom alone belongs the issues of life and death, I fly to Thee for mercy. Look generously upon me, O Lord, and the more the outward woman decayeth strengthen me, I beseech Thee. So much the more continually with Thy grace and Holy Spirit. In the inner woman give me unfeigned repentance for all the errors of my past life, and steadfast faith in Thy Son Jesus, that my sins be done away by Thy mercy, and my pardon sealed in Heaven before I go hence, and be seen no more. As my dissolution draweth near so fit and prepare me against the hour of death that after my departure hence in peace, and in Thy favour my soul may be received in Thine everlasting Kingdom through Jesus Christ our Lord. Amen.*

The 139th Psalm, 7th to the 13th verse, which Martha urges Otto to read, may have been a special message to her love:

*Whither shall I go from thy spirit? Or whither shall I flee from thy presence?*

*If I ascent up into heaven, thou art there: if I make my bed in hell, behold, thou art there.*

*If I take wings of the morning, and dwell in the uttermost parts of the sea; Even there shall thy hand lead me, and thy right hand shall hold me.*

*If I say, Surely the darkness shall cover me; even the night shall be light about me.*

*Yea, the darkness hideth not from thee; but the night shineth as the day; the darkness and the light are both alike to thee.*

*For though has possessed my reins: thou has covered me in my mother's womb.*

Martha was accompanied by Mrs Hutchinson, a salvation army worker, up until the morning of her hanging. Martha allegedly said to her, 'I freely forgive all who have injured me, as I hope to be forgiven.' She later had the ministrations of Reverend Scott and his assistant Reverend Forbes, who still tried to gain a last-minute confession.

Then just before 10 am on 22<sup>nd</sup> October, the Sherriff Mr Ellis and his Deputy Mr Casey came to the scaffold cell and Ellis said 'I demand the body of Martha Needle.' Martha was then claimed by the Sherriff's assistants, and led to the scaffold, accompanied by Ellis and Casey, the Governor of the Gaol, Reverend Scott, Captain Burrowes, the Chief Medical Officer Dr Shield, a few reporters, and Justices of the Peace.[161]

Her slight body, around 50 kg, was covered by a brown wincey dress weighted by lead to prevent ballooning and fixed with a cord, and by a death cap on her head to hide the hideousness of the event. The hangman, Roberts, strapped down her hands and slipped the hemp noose over her head,

---

The Argus, 23rd October 1894

and deftly adjusted the knot.[162] As Martha stepped up to the scaffold, she was given a final opportunity to speak.

'Do you have anything to say?' asked Sheriff Ellis.

Martha said firmly but almost inaudibly, 'No Sir. I have nothing to say.' She had already woken early to write her last important messages to her beloved Otto.

The bolt was drawn and the platform door sprung open as Martha suddenly fell eight foot. The hanging was described as efficient and going without a hitch, with death occurring instantaneously. After an hour, her body was removed and Dr Youl held the usual formal inquest. A 'death mask,' a plaster cast of her face, was made after her death, as was the custom. This would have attracted the interest of phrenologists of the time keen to study the skulls of criminals, and sometimes phrenologists attended executions. This cast is currently on display at the Old Melbourne Gaol museum.

At sunset, Martha's body was buried in quicklime in the grounds of the Gaol. Reverend Scott recited prayers as she was buried. A bluestone brick with her initials carved into it marked the date of death and the approximate spot of where Martha was buried. This brick was subsequently used in the building of a sea wall at Brighton in Victoria.

\*

The issue of whether Martha was penitent about the murders was much debated even after her death. Nowadays, the remorse of the accused is taken into account by judges when sentencing. Reverend Scott, his assistant Forbes and Mrs Hutchinson all saw Martha before she went to the scaffold,

---

162  The Weekly Times, 27th October 1894

but they had very different opinions about Martha and her penitence. Reverend Scott waxed lyrically to the press about the character of Martha, saying that she was a 'psychological enigma' who showed a lack of feeling about the murders:

*From the time I first saw her I considered her an abnormal woman. She had a masterful will, a vast fund of vanity and a passionate nature...She was uninstructed, but had a good deal of native tact and kept her ignorance from being apparent by a ready wit, an agreeable manner, and the fascination of a not uncomely person...Martha Needle was a psychological conundrum, and as such was well worthy of the close study of mental scientists, moral philosophers and students of criminology. She may have been as infamous as she has been portrayed, but the question arose: How came she so? Were the horrible qualities attributed to her inherent and hereditary or were they contracted, cultivated and made potent by the environment? ...The unhappy woman not only made no confession to me in the cell on Monday, but when I spoke to her she again maintained that she was perfectly innocent of the charge of murder. I never saw anyone so inflexible and persistent, and so hardened against softer influences.'*

*The Weekly Times, 27th October 1894*

This perspective that Martha was without remorse was also carried in the religious *Truth and Progress* newspaper. However, Mrs Hutchinson, had gained an entirely different perspective from her last hours with Martha:

*'I was with her from an early house this morning, and I remained until the chaplain came to her.'*

'How did you find her this morning?'

'Very soft and penitent. She was softer than she has ever been before since she was sentenced.'

As this did not correspond with the chaplain's account, a further question was put to make the matter clearer.

'Of course,' said Mrs Hutchinson, 'the chaplain saw her later than I did, and probably knows more about her state at the last moment: but then I think she would be more likely to show her real feelings towards a woman. I tried to make her realise the terrible position in which she stood, whilst at the same time being gentle and sympathetic to her.'

'You believe, then, that she felt her position?'

'Yes, I really believe she did. But she was not an ordinary woman in the matter of displaying feelings. She had a peculiar reserve of manner, and would hide her real self from people.'

'You said she was penitent, Mrs Hutchinson, but she does not seem to have shown penitence in a very marked manner.'

'Well, I will tell you this – my own observation of her leads me to the belief that she was a woman without any intelligent apprehension of what most people consider the most serious things in life...She seemed to be wrongly balanced in some way, and, as I have said, did not seem to realise the seriousness of things which most people regard as the most solemn things in life.'

Otto was furious when he read about Reverend Scott's behaviour toward Martha the night before and the morning of her death, and he promptly wrote to *The Argus* to put matters straight. The newspaper reported they had received a letter from Otto, where he swore that he did not tell the Reverend he believed Martha to be guilty. Otto did not wish to discuss this matter until Reverend Scott's reply to Otto's letters, but he wished to convey to *The Argus* that he was certain that Martha Needle was in fact penitent. *The Weekly Times* visited Otto Juncken after Martha's hanging to find out more about the dispute between Otto and Reverend Scott: the newspaper falsely claimed that Otto told their reporter that Martha was innocent of the crimes. Another letter from Otto to his mother – allegedly released by Mrs Juncken to the SA *Advertiser* newspaper – was published in *The Argus* on the 30th October, in which Otto allegedly spoke of Martha's 'evil' and her being 'so utterly depraved that she has not the ordinary feeling of the human being.' The supposed letter from Otto also stated 'had things gone smoothly with us from the first, there is no doubt that I would have followed the two little girls…bad as things are for you all, my dear mother, they might have been worse.' It was unclear if this letter was actually written by Otto. There were also newspaper rumours that Otto had gone missing, and was suspected of having made an attempt on his life.

Otto finally had the last words on the matter when the paper owned by his brother-in-law, John Jones (married to his older sister Emma), the *Port Adelaide News and LeFevre Peninsula Advertiser*, which had largely been silent on the Richmond Poisoning Case, published the following letter. Neither the Adelaide or Melbourne newspapers picked up on its content.

*The Richmond Poisoning Case*

*Many people are under a wrong impression as regards Otto Juncken's conduct towards Mrs. Needle, but the following letter, dated October 24th, 1894, and written to his sister at Lyndoch, will put quite a different aspect on the whole affair to that which has been given in the other newspapers: -*

'I am glad that you received no news prior to the receipt of my message, to the effect that I was missing. Of course you will know all about it by now and see how utterly absurd the rumour was; still, a lot is made at times over such a thing, and I was afraid that you would have heard it and would think that there was at least some truth in it. I know that you all and everyone know that I have more strength of mind and determination of character than to be prompted to do myself an injury over a thing like this. Ten such troubles centred into one would not have any such effect on me. It is an undoubtedly bitter thing for me to bear. I had hoped that with last Monday's tragic ending all necessity for any explanations would have been over. However, an event took place on Sunday night which has caused me to receive the trouble afresh. How sorry I am that it is so I can not tell you, but my feelings as a man forced me to take the steps I have done. Of course you will know that in her last days she sent for me, and in a Christian spirit I visited her several times. Those visits I have no hesitation in saying, were the means of making the woman see and feel her position more than anything else. I know her nature, and that kindness, sympathy and forgiveness for anything she may have wronged me in, would be only the paving stones to her true repentance. I did not wish to have to allude to anything of this kind, but I must in a measure explain myself. Her whole being and existence were centred in the one thing – her strong passion for me – and I could plainly see that by proper handling of that feeling she could be made a penitent woman* *and die with the peace and forgiveness of God in her heart. That she did so I am confident of; for more than a fortnight before the end I felt that the woman was quite prepared to die, and my mind felt comforted in the thought that I, by my kind heartedness, had been the means of bringing her to a truly penitent state. Her last letter to me, by which you will by this time have no doubt read, and which I received the day after the execution, has quite assured me as to her true state of mind as at the last. The chaplain of the gaol tried hard to get her to confess, although he now flatly denies that he did so. He put it to me that I was the only barrier to a confession, and wished me to go and tell her that I believed she had committed the crimes with a full knowledge of what she was doing. He argued that this was her last prop – her faith and confidence in me – and that taken from her she would break down completely and confess to all. He told me that he did not wish for the confession for her spiritual wellbeing, that could be attained without any confession to a man, but he wanted to make it public, to satisfy the minds of the jury, one of whom was a personal friend of his – to satisfy them as to whether they were justified in their verdict. I told him that I was satisfied in my own mind that she was penitent and quite prepared to meet her God, and as he required the confession solely for the minds of the jury and to justify them in their verdict, I could be of no assistance to him, the whole thing should have been quite clear to the jury, and had they had a doubt on the matter, she should have received the benefit of it. The fact of me telling her an untruth, as I should have had to do to have done as Mr. Scott wished to me, believing as I do that she has no knowledge of the acts, would have had the effect of breaking her down in spirits completely without having the desired effect, even if she had full knowledge of all the acts that she had perpetrated. A confession could never be extorted from a woman like her by such unfair means. If kindness and loving ministrations would not extract it, it could never be done by harshness, so I absolutely refused to do what he wished. What did he do? On Sunday night, when he thought that I would not have the chance of refuting his assertion, he told her that I and all of her friends believed that she had committed all those crimes wilfully, knowingly, and maliciously. He now denies that he did so. He says that he added that – "I believed her to have done the acts but was not conscious of what she had done." This is false, he did not say so, and I can bring forward incontestable proof to that effect. She knew my feelings on the subject, I had stated them in the witness box, and I have also told her since on more than one occasion that the evidence was so clear against her that it could not be pushed aside, and that I believed she had committed the acts but was innocent of any knowledge of them. So if Mr. Scott told her what he now says he did, he only told her what she already knew, and how can he explain the passionate outburst of feeling that the woman gave vent to. For it was a diabolical scheme on his part to extort a confession from an unhappy wretch in the last few hours of her life (when he, as a minister of God, should have been consoling and comforting her and reconciling her to her doom) by taking her the comfort that had sustained the unhappy woman through all that terrible trial – the knowledge that I was at all events and satisfied enough to give her the benefit of the doubt. What right had that man to make use of my name in the manner he did. I refused to do so myself, and I gave him no authority to do so. I have taken him to task over the matter, and I feel I have done only my duty as a man of independence of thought and action. You need not be in the least afraid that I will get myself into trouble or disgrace myself over the whole matter. I think and feel assured that I have the public sympathy, everyone is indignant that such means should have been resorted to. However, I do not after today intend to take any further notice or action in the matter. I cannot tell you how this has worried me, I think I have felt more keenly over this than all of Monday's terrible work. She was quite resigned to her end and I was content that matters should be as they were, it was the best possible thing that could have happened for all concerned.'*

Port Adelaide News and Le Fevre Peninsula Advertiser,
November 1894

Far from his life being over, after the death of Martha, Otto continued to live in Richmond and married Bertha Albrecht in 1901 and had six children. Always known as a hard worker, Otto redeemed himself for any guilt associated with the death of his brother Louis or attempted murder of Herman, through devotion to his work. In 1918, Otto changed the spelling of his surname to Yuncken, and teamed up with Lauritz Hansen to start one of the most successful construction businesses in Australia which continues today, Hansen and Yuncken. This business has been responsible for building many important buildings in Victoria (including the National Bank, Port Authority, Myer building and The Age building) and throughout Australia. Modern buildings built by the company include the Waterfront City, Victoria, Adelaide Casino, Commonwealth Law Courts, South Australia and the old and new Royal Adelaide Hospitals. Otto Juncken never spoke of Martha Needle and the story of The Richmond Poisoning Case was not passed down through the family. After Martha's hanging, the rest of Otto's life was lived out in physical manifestations of redemption.

Contemporary newspapers continued to publish on the case well after Martha was hanged. The New Zealand press was particularly dramatic and satirical in reporting the exploits of her life and death, finding her crimes far worse than that of babyfarmer Frances Knorr.

*In the Melbourne Gaol recently Mrs Martha Needle, pressed by circumstances and a cord, retired from active life, leaving a void in the toxicological business which it will be difficult to fill.*

*Bay of Plenty Times, Vol XX11, Issue 3201, 30<sup>th</sup>*
*November 1894*

*The crimes for which Mrs Needle suffered are far and away worse than those that brought Frances Knorr to the gallows. Martha Needle was a cold blooded poisoner. Husband, paramour, and her own children all fell victims to her extraordinary human suffering.*

*One would have thought that this inhuman monster would have stopped in her awful work of murder...So [through] the patient investigation made by Superintendent Brown, an exceptionally smart detective officer, and Superintendent Whitney, one of his assistants, the cruel and diabolic deeds of this she devil were brought to light.*

*Wanganui Herald, Vol XXV111, Issue 8615, 26<sup>th</sup>*
*October 1894*

The belief that Martha was a skilled, ruthless and conniving poisoner fully cognisant of her deeds was a predominant theme in the press. *The Wanganui Herald* erroneously claimed that the warder who spent her last hours with Martha was a 'lifer' who had herself killed her first husband and had 'just as great a respect and admiration for the secret art of poisoning.' The notion that being a poisoner was a skilled and secret art, could be found in a medical text from the 1840s:

> *The crime of poisoning from its nature must always be a secret one. It seems to have escaped the attention of those who have written on the subject that the practice of such an art requires the knowledge, not only of a dexterous toxicologist, but also of a skillful physician, for success must depend on the exact imitation of some natural cause.*
>
> Robert Christinson, MD, 1844

*

Some elements of the press were of the opinion that Martha had been too ambitious in her crimes and attempted just one life too many.

> *Save for her callous and daring attempt upon the life of Herman Juncken, Mrs Needle would now be at large and as free from suspicion as any ordinary member of the community.*
>
> The Argus, 29th September, 1894

It appeared that Martha was successful in covering up her crimes due to the incompetence of the various medical professionals around her, the nascence of the field of psychiatry, as well as the way she presented: as a charming woman, who showed great care towards those who had fallen ill around her. The more her loved ones suffered, the more 'caring' she would appear towards them, when she had actually poisoned them, with symptoms of their illness abating and returning. Martha was also reportedly cooperative with doctors and keen to get a second opinion. Was it because of the attention that she was seeking and receiving that she continued on the path of her heinous crimes? The slow and sporadic poisoning of her loved ones might suggest that she had what was formerly known as Munchausen Syndrome by proxy – now known as factitious disorder imposed upon another – where illness or injury may be caused by a person who is meant to be providing caregiving. She received a great deal of attention and sympathy from the community throughout their illness and deaths, and especially from her beloved Otto.

It appears from her death mask that Martha may have suffered from Fetal Alcohol Syndrome – due to her features, which would not be surprising given that her mother was in and out of the Adelaide gaol for drunkenness. One of the key physical features of Fetal Alcohol Syndrome is 'a smooth ridge between the upper lip and nose, small and wide-set eyes, a very thin upper lip, or other abnormal facial features.'[163] Behavioural symptoms include aggression and difficulty controlling anger, antisocial behaviour, impulsivity and mood swings – behaviours which Martha had displayed.

The sexual abuse Martha experienced from her step-father Daniel Foran and physical violence from both parents could also help to explain her volatile temperament, problems with

---

163 Fetal alcohol syndrome. https://www.healthline.com/health/fetal-alcohol-syndrome

mental health and a pattern of abuse that was to be repeated throughout Martha's life. Whilst most people who experience such abuse would not end up committing the kind of crimes that Martha did, such a difficult early start could help to explain her vulnerability to being in a violent relationship. It is now thought that family and peer support can buffer the impact of abuse,[164] but young Martha seemed to have no one to turn to, with an unreliable, often imprisoned mother, and her older sisters in the Destitute Asylum and then out on service in country regions.

The report of the religious South Australian newspaper *Truth and Progress* took a more compassionate position on the case than other contemporary newspapers. The paper appeared to be aware of the background of Martha and her family.

*The saddest reflection in the sad story, whose last chapter has just ended, is that a person can be so led on by sin and feel so little as to its consequences. Its development is not confined to one person, the process is carried on from one generation to another till a monster is produced, who is deprived of ordinary human feeling. Thus while Martha Needle could have received grace to overcome the bad traits of her character, she was not alone to blame for her disposition. She and multitudes besides have started in the race of life heavily handicapped, and in the final decision those who have been the cause of this will not be held guiltless.*

*Truth and Progress, Nov 1, 1894*

---

164  AIFS (2013). The long-term effects of child sexual abuse CFCA Paper No. 11 – January 2013

Amongst the evidence in the Martha Needle case were clues suggesting what might now be called a dissociative state, specifically depersonalisation disorder or 'derealisation' where 'people may feel they have lost contact with external reality: that their home, workplace, friends or relatives are unfamiliar or strange. The experience of derealisation often involves a failure to recognise familiar objects and people.[165] Evidence of 'derealisation' or 'depersonalisation' occurred when Martha did not recognise Otto or refused to believed that her mother was her real mother. It can result from traumatic events such as the severe physical and sexual abuse experienced by Martha as a child. Dissociation and post-traumatic stress disorder symptoms can also be part of suffering domestic violence as an adult, for instance 'battered wife syndrome' and can contribute to post-traumatic stress disorder or Borderline Personality Disorder[166] which is a possibility, based on reports of Martha's mood swings, uncontrolled outbursts, suicidal intentions, and her extremely charming qualities. Martha may have also had a dissociative identity disorder which is associated with 'frequent gaps in personal history that are not adequately explained by ordinary forgetfulness and may span in duration from minutes to years as 'alters' take control of behaviour.'[167]

It was difficult to comprehend how Martha was apparently so deeply affected by the loss of her children and at the same time pursued an infatuation with the gentle Otto. Perhaps this was also a sign of her dissociation. The court trials indicated that Martha often complained of pain in the head, was often in a comatose state for hours, and could be heard speaking to her deceased husband and children: these might be the

---

165  Collins, F. (2004). What is dissociation? Dissociation Australia.
166  Ibid
167  Ibid

effects of acute psychosis associated with a disorder such as schizophrenia, or chlorodyne addiction.

As the police raided the Bridge Road residence, Martha had attempted to take the contents of a bottle of chlorodyne kept in her bedroom, suggesting evidence that Martha took the drug. During the 19th century, chlorodyne was a common home remedy for a range of ailments. Originally developed to fight cholera, it had a high opiate content and thus was a common cause of addiction and deaths through overdose. It was a readily available sedative and analgesic; a concoction of laudanum, morphine hydrochloride, cannabis and chloroform. It was used as a 'cure all' for pain relief, coughs, colds, bronchitis, colic, asthma, consumption (pulmonary tuberculosis), indigestion, insomnia, migraines, neuralgia, neuropathy, diphtheria, fever, croup, diarrhoea, dysentery, epilepsy, hysteria, palpitations, spasms, rheumatism, gout, cancer, toothache and meningitis.[168] Chlorodyne also led to hallucinations and falling unconscious. An article in the *British Medical Journal* of 1963 reports on three cases of chlorodyne addiction, where all three patients had been unconscious several times because of chlorodyne and one of these had been in a coma and admitted to hospital eight times; in two of these cases the patient was acutely psychotic with auditory and visual hallucinations and paranoid delusions. The same article refers to a fourth case where an addicted person had been acutely psychotic, with visual and auditory hallucinations.[169] Other symptoms included neurological effects

---

168 Various sources: Advertisement for chlorodyne: https://teara.govt.nz/en/zoomify/39556/advertisement-for-chlorodyne chlorodyne: https://en.wikipedia.org/wiki/Chlorodyne The Oldie: https://www.theoldie.co.uk/article/oldie-life-what-was-chlorodyne 10 Old Timey medicines that got people high: https://www.alternet.org/drugs/10-old-timey-medicines-got-people-high Chlorodyne, Collins English Dictionary: https://www.collinsdictionary.com/dictionary/english/chlorodyne Herb Museum: http://www.herbmuseum.ca/content/chlorodyne

(buzzing in the ears, pins and needles and weakness in the limbs). Whatever her mental condition, Martha would have been unlikely to have been convicted if using the 'product rule,' whereby her acts may have been seen to be 'the 'product' of a mental disease or 'defect:' this rule does not exist in Australia, and determinations of criminal insanity are largely based upon the 150-year-old McNaughton rules.[170]

*

Martha Needle was survived by her mother and step-father, two half-brothers and two sisters. In 1895, Martha's brother John, aged 23 years, married Elizabeth Downer, aged 17 years, at her father's residence at Hilton. He was a contractor and labourer who continued to live at Hilton[171] and became a successful builder and publican in his later life, building many of the houses in the inner western suburbs, and passing on a small fortune to his descendants.

Mary and Daniel Foran both spent a great deal of time in the Destitute Asylum, in courts and in gaol. In March 1900, then aged 63, Mary Foran was again charged with 'drunken, idle and disorderly' behaviour. On another occasion charged for the same offence she said that she was a 'highland lady' and earned her living by knitting and telling fortunes. She was sent to the Adelaide Gaol for two months. In 1906, Mary died, aged 69 years of age.

---

169 Conlon, M.F. (1963). Addiction to Chlorodyne, British Medical Journal. 9th November, 1963.

170 Prosono 1994:21, cited in Shea, P. (2001). M'Naghten Revisited -Back to the Future? (The Mental Illness Defence, A Psychiatric Perspective). Current Issues in Criminal Justice, vol 12, no 3.

171 John Foran was a Labourer living at Bagot Street (now Avenue), Hilton in 1903 (Wise Directory).

In November 1903, Daniel Foran senior was again arrested in Adelaide and charged with indecently assaulting a young girl, the case being dismissed in the Adelaide Police Court. Perhaps natural justice prevailed when Daniel was drunk and knocked down by a 'Try Again'[172] bus in 1909.[173] At the time he was admitted to hospital, with the hospital notes reading, 'Quite destitute, has no home.' He discharged himself but later returned, probably because of his homelessness, with the hospital recording 'He left care on his instinct, but had to return.' He claimed that he was over a hundred years of age when he died in 1927 at The Nursing Sisters' Hospital in North Adelaide, however according to his military records he was born around 1838 and only 89 years of age. An astonishing obituary appeared in the *SA Register* which gives some indication of how he portrayed himself:

*Mr. Daniel Foran died at the Nursing Sisters' Hospital, North Adelaide, on Sunday. He had been at the institution for several years and was described as "a wonderful centenarian" being 101 years of age. Mr. Foran was born at Carrickaneach, a few miles from Limerick, Ireland, and in 1855 he enlisted in the 40th (Somersetshire) Regiment of the British Army. After being at several army stations for some years, the regiment was ordered to Melbourne, and Mr. Foran was one of the company that sailed in the ship*

---

172  This is likely to refer to Spring Carts. As stated by the State Library of South Australia, 'Prior to the opening of the railway to Port Adelaide the mode of transport to the Port was by spring carts. These started from King William Street, thence to Morphett Street, the driver calling out, 'Port, Sir'. If a load was not forthcoming the driver would return to King William Street and repeat the procedure. Then, on the second try, if a load was still absent he would return again and say, 'As there is no load you must get out and wait for an hour.' http://www.slsa.sa.gov.au/manning/sa/trans/coaches.htm

173  The Advertiser, 24th June 1909

*Windsor. He had some experience on the goldfields and for a time was quartered with a portion of his regiment in Adelaide. Eventually he took his discharge in Melbourne, and returned to South Australia. For some time he was employed on sheep stations in the vicinity of Port Lincoln and Fowler's Bay. He was later in the service of the Surveyor General of the day (Mr. Goyder), by whom he was employed as a handyman at home, and as a ganger on various surveying expeditions. He was then in the service of Col. Makin for 16 or 17 years.[174] He was also said to have been servant to various people in North Adelaide for about 40 years. One of his employers was a son of Governor Gawler, who lived in Childers street. Prior to entering the hospital, suffering from a skin disease, in 1923; he had found employment as a caretaker. Mr. Foran's wife died some time ago in the Adelaide Hospital. Of his five sons,[175] two died at Port Lincoln, another is buried in West Terrace and another at Wallaroo.*

*SA Register, 11ᵗʰ January 1927*

The casualties of Daniel Foran not only included his step-daughter Martha who was 31 when she was hanged, but also included his son Daniel Foran junior, who died at 35 years of age when living at Alford. Long estranged from his family, at aged 29 years, he was apprehended at Port Wakefield in 1895 and sent to the Parkside Lunatic Asylum for two weeks.[176] Daniel junior was charged with being drunk when aged 34

---

174  A well-known soldier who started the voluntary military movement in SA: The Advertiser, 3ʳᵈ November, 1924.
175  Possibly should read five children, including step-daughter Martha, Daniel Junior, John, Margaret and George.
176  The South Australian Police Gazette, August 14, 1895.

years of age, and sent to the Adelaide Gaol for two months. He was later picked up at Port Adelaide and again sent to the lunatic asylum. In 1902, he died drunk in a prison cell at the copper mining town of Wallaroo,[177] near Alford on the northern Yorke Peninsula:

*A PRISON CELL MYSTERY. Wallaroo, March 29, 1902*

*Daniel Foran was brought into Wallaroo yesterday from Alford, and handed over to the police. He was acting strangely, and Dr. Fulton attended him in the police - cell this morning, in the presence of the police and Mr. James Malcolm, who came to hold an enquiry. Some time afterwards Foran died, and an inquest will be held tomorrow. Dr. Fulton at the request of Mr. Malcolm will conduct a post-mortem examination this afternoon. Deceased was at times a heavy drinker. He called at Mr. Mudge's farm, Tickera, and told them he wanted to give himself up to the police. The last words he mentioned this morning were, "I did not do it."*

The jury of the inquiry into this death returned the following verdict: "The said Daniel Foran came to his death by failure of the heart's action, accelerated by self-abuse and reckless living." The coroner commended the police for their great kindness to the deceased while in the cell – kindness that he had been little afforded during his life.

---

177  The Advertiser, 22nd March 1900, pg.3

# 9

# Epilogue

Martha Needle's case highlights the lack of understanding of, and responses to, child abuse and mental illness in the 19th century and their effects, and the plight of poor women and children in early colonial Australia. It also sheds light on current issues of poverty, domestic and family violence, responses to mental illness and the treatment of children, including in government institutions and the justice system.

Excessive family poverty provided the context for Martha's crimes. Much has been made of Australia being the 'lucky country' for immigrants, but how lucky was it for poor women and children? For Mary Charles (nee Newland) and the next generations born into poverty[178] in Australia, economic circumstances were very poor and there was little public assistance. Women in the 19th century were heavily dependent upon their spouses financially and lost legal rights with marriage (and any earnings were given to their husband). They usually remained with spouses, even if they were 'unlucky' to have

---

178 New research suggests that it takes four generations to reach the average wage if one is born into poverty, see: Liddy, M. (2018). Chart of the day: If you're born poor, it takes until your great-great grandchildren to overcome it. ABC http://www.abc.net.au/news/2018-07-23/chart-of-the-day-oecd-generational-poverty/9997970

married the likes of a 'blackguard' such as Daniel Foran. Between 1859 and 1899 there were less than ten applicants for divorce or legal separation in South Australia[179] and even in 1901, the crude divorce rate in Australia was just 0.1 per 1000.[180] Under the South Australian Matrimonial Causes Act 1858, women were required to prove two grounds for divorce (whilst men only had to prove one), such as their husband's adultery and cruelty or drunkenness.[181]

The crimes of Martha Needle attracted much contemporary and subsequent attention from the press and public (women in particular), perhaps due to the crimes being contrary to the strong emphasis on caring and the mothering role for women in society. This led to challenges in understanding why Martha committed her crimes, and especially why she killed her children – from outward appearances, she seemed to be a devoted mother, but in reality, she was a heartless killer with no ordinary level of feeling or empathy. The attention that the *Richmond Poisoning Case* attracted brought especial concern to the editor of the religious *Truth and Progress* newspaper.

*It is a pity anyhow that a murderer cannot be punished in some effectual way without attaining to such notoriety as is invariably the case. The last criminal has been kept before the public for many months. Her every word, action, and look have been daily chronicled as if of great importance, till diseased minds are in danger of regarding her as a heroine worthy of imitation, tragic end and all.*

179  Adelaidia, Marriage and Divorce. http://adelaidia.sa.gov.au/subjects/marriage-and-divorce
180  AIFS. (2018). Divorce in Australia. Source data. https://aifs.gov.au/facts-and-figures/divorce-australia/divorce-australia-source-data
181  Adelaidia, op cit.

Was the *Truth and Progress* prophetic? Was murderer Alexander Newland Lee seeking the same sort of notoriety as that of his Auntie Martha, The Richmond Poisoner? It seems that the combination of dire poverty, financial stress, domestic violence and perhaps psychopathic character contributed to the same murderous events occurring within the same family a generation later.

Concerns about widespread copycat murders arising from publicity have not been borne out. We have seen a 'true crime spree' on television and in newspapers and books in present times however, in Australia at least, homicides rates have been dropping. This is even the case in South Australia where serial killer Martha was bred: despite Adelaide's reputation as being the 'murder capital' of the world, South Australia has one of the lowest murder rates in the country and the world.

However, it is more likely that an Australian will be murdered by someone that they know than by the hands of a serial killer. Additionally, the proportion of homicide associated with intimate partner violence in Australia has worryingly increased, and one woman dies every week from domestic violence,[182] which needs to be urgently addressed. The high rates of lifetime domestic and family violence experienced in our community (especially among our Aboriginal and Torres Strait Islander population) are associated with child abuse. When it was suggested that Harry Needle was violent towards Martha, the newspapers at the time suggested that it was a 'natural response' by a jealous man towards a flirty and 'flighty' character. Attitudes have come a long way in the past century, but not far enough. We need a greater focus on prevention of domestic, family and sexual violence, the prevention of all forms of child

---

182 AIHW. (2018). Family, domestic and sexual violence in Australia. 2018. Australian Institute of Health and Welfare, Canberra.

abuse and the institutionalisation of children by governments, responses to child safety and the protection of children's rights. This will entail ongoing efforts towards changing attitudes and values towards domestic and family violence.

Whilst women are more likely to be victims of intimate partner violence and males perpetrators, research into murder-suicide has found that victims of male offenders are more likely to be intimate partners, whilst victims of female offenders were more likely to be children.[183] This was interpreted by the researcher as meaning that for those women with the intention to die by suicide who commit murder suicide, they continue to act out the responsibilities of the mothering role in a perverse way.[184] But in the case of Martha Needle her children, husband and brother-in-law suffered for months as she administered poison to them, suggesting that she was profoundly disturbed.

The descriptions of Martha's mental health status and symptoms, including hallucinations, catatonia, fainting fits and failure to recognise her beloved Otto, point toward a severe mental illness, however this was not fully explored by her legal defence or the court. When it was introduced and her case lobbied for at the highest level, the decision had been made and the Governor was reluctant to overturn this, probably due to public representations and perceptions of Martha. It might be said that there was deplorable treatment and lack of understanding of mental health in 19th century colonial Australia. However, many people with a mental health condition, both women and men, still end up in the justice system for exhibiting signs of mental illness or responding

183 Barnes, J. Murder followed by suicide in Australia, 1973-1992: a research note. Journal of Sociology 2000: 36; 1.
184 Ibid.

unpredictably when police are called out; some still ultimately pay with their lives. In 2018, it was reported that half of those shot by police in New South Wales had a mental illness.[185] On a positive note, Australian courts have adopted therapeutic jurisprudence, which emerged from the field of mental health law. These principles and practices consider behavioural sciences in order that courts have a beneficial effect on the psychological wellbeing of clients whilst meeting due process requirements. Nevertheless, high numbers of people with mental health conditions in the justice and corrections system internationally, low awareness of mental health symptoms and conditions across the community, and a lack of adequate judicial, treatment and community based support services continue to be problematic.

A factor of legal interest in this case was the all-male jury, with women only first appearing on juries in Australia in the 1920s. Currently recognised is the role that female jurors can have in jury decision making, particularly when it comes to sexual offences: one study showed that females on the jury increased conviction rates by 16 per cent.[186] Another legal point of interest in this story is the experiences of child witnesses in court: 12 year old Martha, and nine year old Danny reporting on the abuse of Martha, and eight year old Amelia Lee giving evidence in the murder trial of her father. It is now recognised that children can be significantly traumatised by providing evidence in court, and that they require tailored support and information.[187] No such support

---

185  Kate Wild, Greg Miskelly and Giselle Wakatama. (2018). 'A potent, tragic, fatal mix': More than half of people shot dead by NSW Police have a mental illness. ABC News: 5 Mar 2018, 2:38pm http://www.abc.net.au/news/ 2018-03-05/police-shootings-and-mental-health-a-potent-tragic-fatal-mix/ 9493356

186  Hjalmarsson, R & Bayer, P. (2016). How women change outcomes in courtrooms and beyond, The Conversation, February 29th 2016.

would have been available to the children in this story at the time. The treatment of neglected and abused children generally was terrible – the solution to Martha's problems was to be sent off to work as a domestic servant when she was 12 years old, whilst her brothers went to the industrial school and other similar children were sent to a leaking hulk off Largs Bay.

In Martha's case, she experienced extreme abuse by her parents and the alcohol addiction of at least one if not both of her parents. Protections for children in Australia were in their infancy in the 1890s, after the era of the worst cases of 'babyfarming,' with the establishment of boarding out societies and other charities. But Martha and her siblings' story of childhood abuse and its long-term effects and the development of protections for children is very much a current one. Whilst the majority of those who suffer from such terrible abuse may go on to live productive and meaningful lives, child abuse, its prevention, and public responses to its effects are unresolved matters in contemporary Australian society. One hundred and forty-six years after MacKillop's excommunication for report-ing child sexual abuse in the Catholic Church, Australia's royal commission into institutional responses to child sexual abuse (2017) highlighted inappropriate responses to abuse, and a redress scheme has just been established (2018). The acting head of the catholic church in Adelaide recently announced that a new child protection law requiring priests to report child abuse revealed in confession would not apply to them.[188] One hundred and thirty two years after the Way Commission in South Australia recommended institutionalising children as a last

---

187 See: 'Seen and heard: priority for children in the legal process (ALRC Report 84).'
188 The Advertiser, June 15th, 2008.

resort, it is astounding to think that detention and abuse of children in state, territory and Australian government and state sponsored institutions and care arrangements still occurs.[189]

---

189 The extremely harsh punishment and breach of the rights of children recently led to the Royal Commission into the Protection and Detention of Children in the Northern Territory which further uncovered examples of the abuse of (primarily Indigenous) children within detention.

# 10

# Acknowledgements

I wish to thank Tammy Martin and Marg Albrechtsen who kindly provided me with genealogical records and information on Martha Needle and Alexander Lee, and Otto (deceased) and Bart Yuncken for assistance and providing permission for including the letters in the PROV/Australian Manuscripts Collection, State Library of Victoria file on Martha Needle. I also would like to thank the volunteers and staff at the South Australian Genealogical and Heraldry Society (now Genealogy SA), the Genealogical Society of Victoria (Beverley Spinks), Friends of Boroondara (Kew) Cemetery (Cathie Shaw), State Library of Victoria (Lucy Shedden), Sandringham District Historical Society (Margaret Tripp) and the Public Record Office of Victoria (Helen D. Harris OAM) for assistance with research. I acknowledge the original source (State Library of Victoria, Public Record Office of Victoria) and newspaper material used throughout (National Library of Australia, Newspapers Trove and Papers Past, NZ), particularly when referring to the court trials. Thanks to the resources and support of the Geneva Writers' Group and Writers SA. Thanks to Raelene Linden, Dr Malcolm Riley and Jessica Carr for reading an early version of the manuscript and providing advice, and to Dr Pierre-Alain Wulser for encouragement and calculation of 'grains to grams.' Also thank you to Glenda Downing for providing assessment and advice on the manuscript, and to Jessica Stewart for structural and copyediting the manuscript, Jessica Carr for proofreading and Joel Noam, Critical Mass, for managing the publishing process.

# 11

# References

Books, journal articles and reports:

Australian Law Reform Commission. (1997). *Seen and heard: priority for children in the legal process.* (ALRC Report 84).

Abnet et al., (2005). Tooth loss is associated with increased risk of total death and death from upper gastrointestinal cancer, heart disease, and stroke in a Chinese population-based cohort, *International Journal of Epidemiology*, Volume 34, Issue 2, 1 April 2005, Pages 467–474.

Australian Institute of Health and Welfare. (2018). Family, domestic and sexual violence in Australia. 2018. AIHW, Canberra.

Asokan, T.V. (2016). The insanity defense: Related issues. *Indian J Psychiatry.* 2016 Dec; 58(Suppl 2): S191–S198.

Atkinson & Aveling. (1987). *Australians: A Historical Library: Australians 1838.* Fairfax, Syme & Weldon Associates, NSW, Australia.

Bagot, Charles Hervey (1788–1880), *Australian Dictionary of Biography*, National Centre of Biography, Australian National University, http://adb.anu.edu.au/biography/bagot-charles-hervey-1730/ text1903, published first in hardcopy 1966.

Barnes, J. (2000). Murder followed by suicide in Australia, 1973-1992: a research note. *Journal of Sociology* 2000: 36; 1.

Christinson, R. (1844). *A Treatise of Poisons*, 4th Edition. The Classics of Medicine Library. Birmingham, Alabama: Gryphon Editions; Special Edition 1988, p. 43.

Canon, M. (1993). *Hold Page One, Memoirs of Monty Grover*, Loch Haven Press, Victoria.

Canon, M. (1994). *The woman as murderer: Five who paid with their lives.* Today's Australia Publishing Company, Mornington, Victoria.

Chakravarti, S.N., Faruqi, M.Z & Ganguly, K. R. (1941). Detection of Arsenic in Burnt Human Bones and Ashes, *Indian Medical Gazette*, December 1941.

Dart, R.C. (2004). *Medical toxicology*. Philadelphia: Williams & Wilkins. pp. 1393–1401.

Davison, G, McCarty, J.W., McLeary, A. (eds). *Australians: A Historical Library: Australians 1888*. Fairfax, Syme & Weldon Associates.

Eade, S. 'Spence, Catherine Helen (1825–1910)', *Australian Dictionary of Biography*, National Centre of Biography, Australian National University, http://adb.anu.edu.au/biography/spence-catherine-helen-4627/text7621, published first in hardcopy 1976

Evans, C. (2014). 'Responsibility and criminal law in the late-nineteenth-century British Empire.' *The Howard League for Penal Reform, ECAN Bulletin*, Issue 23, June 2014.

Frost, A. (undated). Kew Historical Society. *Kew in the 1890s depression*. http://kewhistoricalsociety.org.au/khs/wp-content/uploads/Kew-in-the-1890s-Depression-1.pdf

Hjalmarsson, R & Bayer, P. (2016). How women change outcomes in courtrooms and beyond, *The Conversation*, February 29th 2016.

Joshy et al. (2016). Is poor oral health a risk marker for incident cardiovascular disease hospitalisation and all-cause mortality? Findings from 172 630 participants from the prospective 45 and Up Study, *BMJ Open*, 2016; 6(8): e012386.

Kennedy, J. *A Short History of the Parish*. http://www.stmw.org/history-1.html

Kirkwood, D (2006). Elizabeth Scott – the first woman hanged in Victoria, how far have we come? *DVIRC Quarterly*. Edition 1, autumn 2006

McCarthy, S. (2015). *Tom Price: from Stone cutter to Premier*. Wakefield Press. South Australia

Magarey, S. (ed). (2005). *Every yours, C.H.Spence: Catherine Helen Spence's An Autobiography* (1825-1910), Diary (1894) and Some Correspondence (1894-1910). Wakefield Press, Adelaide.

Maudsley, H. Law and Insanity, 1894. *Popular Science Monthly* Volume 5 May 1874. https://en.wikisource.org/wiki/Popular_Science_Monthly/Volume_5/May_1874/Law_and_Insanity

Overington, C. (2014). *Last woman hanged: The terrible true story of Louisa Collins*. Harper Collins Publishers. Sydney.

Pretty, G. 'Wakefield, Edward Gibbon (1796–1862)', Australian Dictionary of Biography, National Centre of Biography, Australian National University, http://adb.anu.edu.au/biography/wakefield-edward-gibbon-2763/text3921, published first in hardcopy 1967

Ratnaike, R N. Acute and chronic arsenic poisoning. Review. Postgraduate Medical Journal. BMJ Journals. Volume 79, Issue 933 https://pmj.bmj.com/content/79/933/391

Schoolmeester WL, White DR. (1980). Arsenic poisoning. South Med J 1980, 73:198–208.

Serle, G. 'Gaunson, David. (1846-1909).' Australian Dictionary of Biography. Australian National University. http://adb.anu.edu.au/biography/gaunson-david-3599

Shea, P. (2001). M'Naghten Revisited -Back to the Future? (The Mental Illness Defence A Psychiatric Perspective). Current Issues in Criminal Justice, vol 12, no 3.

Stratmann, L. (2016). *The Secret Poisoner: A Century of Murder*. Yale University Press.

Whalan D. J. Sir Robert Richard Torrens, *Australian Dictionary of Biography*. Australian National University. Volume 6, (MUP), 1976 http://adb.anu.edu.au/biography/torrens-sir-robert-richard-4739

Wild, K, Miskelly, G, and Wakatama, G. (2018). 'A potent, tragic, fatal mix': More than half of people shot dead by NSW Police have a mental illness. ABC News: 5 Mar 2018, 2:38pm http://www.abc.net.au/news/2018-03-05/police-shootings-and-mental-health-a-potent-tragic-fatal-mix/9493356

Other Publications and Data Base Sources

Adelaide Northern Districts Family History Group (ANDFHG), Newsletter article on Alexander Newland Lee, 5th November 2006.

Collins, F. (2004). What is Dissociation? Dissociation Australia. Pamphlet.

Digger – South Australian Deaths Registrations 1842 to 1915, 1842-1906, 1842-1916.

Melbourne Central Gaol records (Daniel Foran).

Old Melbourne Gaol. The Crown v Edward Kelly, David Gaunson, flier. Old Melbourne Gaol.

Public Record Office of Victoria (prison files and photos of Martha Needle).

Record of the Supreme Court, Adelaide, May sessions 1920, The King against Alexander Newland Lee for Murder. Trial notes of the case of Alexander Newman Lee, Supreme Court of South Australia. Including Witness Statements and Judges concluding notes/speech (78 pages) and Letter addressed to the court, from Mr Alexander Newland Lee.

Scottish Census. 1851 Census, Evie and Rendall, Orkney, Scotland, District no 5.

South Australian Archives. Prisoner Register, Convict Department, Daniel Foran, South Australian archives (vol no 1353)

South Australian Births, deaths and marriages registration office, 1853 record of marriage of Henry Charles and May Newlands, record of marriage of Daniel Foran and May Charles, birth certificate of Martha Needle 1863.

South Australian Police Historical Society, Newsletter article on A.N Lee.

State Library of Victoria. Martha Needle Papers, June 25 – October 16 1894. MS 8296. Australian Manuscripts Collection, State Library of Victoria.

State Library of Victoria. Letters of Administration in the Estate of Henry Needle, Supreme Court of Victoria.

The Richmond Pioneers, Death in the district of East Melbourne, Martha Needle (nee Charles) death notice.

Turnbull, G (ed), Triangle of Tranquillity, 150 years of the Boroondara (Kew) Cemetery 1859-2009. Bridge Rd Richmond, Historical Walk, pamphlet.

Wise Directory, 1903 (SA).


Genealogy SA (formerly South Australian Genealogy and Heraldry Society: SAGHS)

- Royal Adelaide Hospital Records
- Destitute Asylum Records
- Birth and death records
- Catholic Christening, Kapunda No 1011 1859 (Ellen Charles)


Genealogy Society of Victoria

- Research at Genealogy Society of Victoria, undertaken by Beverly Spinks, email received 23rd March 2010 on the Transport vessel, The Windsor


State Records of South Australia

- Old Adelaide Gaol records
- Government of South Australia, State Records, GRG 28/4 Register of cases of destitution
- Government of South Australia. State Records. GRG 28/5 Register of admissions - Destitute Asylum

Websites and online articles by topic:

**Arsenic:**

Agency for toxic substances and disease registry. (2010). Arsenic Toxicity, What are the Physiologic Effects of Arsenic Exposure? https://www.atsdr.cdc.gov/csem/csem.asp?csem=1&po=11

Agency for toxic substances and disease registry. (2018). Health effects of arsenic. https://www.atsdr.cdc.gov/toxprofiles/tp2-c3.pdf

Australian Pesticides and Veterinary Medicines Authority (APVMA). (2014). Arsenic timber treatments. Chemical Review. https://apvma.gov.au/node/12366

Ball, P. (2003). William Morris made Poisonous Wallpaper. Nature. 12th June 2003. https://www.nature.com/news/2003/030612/full/news030609-11.html

Encyclopedia Britannica. Arsenic Poisoning. https://www.britannica.com/science/arsenic-poisoning

Flanders Health Blog. (2016). Arsenic in Wallpaper. 15th December 2016. http://www.flandershealth.us/lead-poisoning/arsenic-in-wallpaper.html

Food Standards Australia New Zealand (2017). Arsenic. http://www.foodstandards.gov.au/consumer/chemicals/arsenic/Pages/default.aspx

Hawksley, L. (2016) Could this Wallpaper kill you? The Telegraph, 7th October 2016. https://www.telegraph.co.uk/books/what-to-read/could-this-wallpaper-kill-you-victorian-britains-lethal-obsessio/

Rae, H. (2016). When Poison was Everywhere, The Atlantic, 11th October 2016. https://www.theatlantic.com/health/archive/2016/10/the-era-when-poison-was-everywhere/503654/

The Smithsonian Magazine. (2017). Arsenic and Old Tastes Make Victorian Wallpaper Deadly, 3rd April 2017: https://www.smithsonianmag.com/smart-news/victorian-wallpaper-got-its-gaudy-colors-poison-180962709/

Taylor's Manual of Medical Jurisprudence, first published 1866. https://archive.org/details/manualofmedicalj00tayl

**Biblical and hymn information:**

Jesus I my cross have taken: http://www.igracemusic.com/hymnbook/hymns/j03.html https://www.youtube.com/watch?v=NhIo2o3WLnA

Henry Francis Lyte: http://www.hymntime.com/tch/bio/l/y/t/lyte_hf.htm

Farewell faithful friends. Scripture Acts 18:21. See: https://hymnary.org/tune/farewell_faithful_friends_we_must_bishop

**Blight/ophthalmia:**

Ball, C, Seeing clearly at the Destitute Asylum – an eyebath, September 20th, 2016. https://migration.history.sa.gov.au/blog/seeing-clearly-at-the-destitute-asylum-an-eyebath/

**Child protection:**

Victorian Children's Aid Society 1893-1991: http://trove.nla.gov.au/people/476814?c=people

**Chlorodyne:**

Alternet. 10 Old Timey medicines that got people high: https://www.alternet.org/drugs/10-old-timey-medicines-got-people-high
Conlon, M.F. (1963). Addiction to Chlorodyne, British Medical Journal. 9th November, 1963.
Chlorodyne: https://en.wikipedia.org/wiki/Chlorodyne
Chlorodyne, Collins English Dictionary: https://www.collinsdictionary.com/dictionary/english/chlorodyne
Herb Museum: http://www.herbmuseum.ca/content/chlorodyne
The Encyclopedia of New Zealand. Advertisement for chlorodyne: https://teara.govt.nz/en/zoomify/39556/advertisement-for-chlorodyne
The Oldie (2017). Oldie Life: What was chlorodyne? December 2017. https://www.theoldie.co.uk/article/oldie-life-what-was-chlorodyne

**Cremation:**

History of Cremation: http://www.ayton.id.au/gary/History/H_cremation.htm

**Divorce:**

Adelaidia, Marriage and Divorce. http://adelaidia.sa.gov.au/subjects/marriage-and-divorce
Australian Institute of Family Studies. (2018). Divorce in Australia. Source data. https://aifs.gov.au/facts-and-figures/divorce-australia/divorce-australia-source-data

**Family History Records:**

Birth and death records. www.ancestry.com.au
Birth and death records. www.findmypast.com.au

Government Gazettes and Sands Directories, World Vital Records (now My Heritage). www.myheritage.com

**Intergenerational poverty:**

Liddy, M. (2018). Chart of the day: If you're born poor, it takes until your great-great grandchildren to overcome it. ABC News. http://www.abc.net.au/news/2018-07-23/chart-of-the-day-oecd-generational-poverty/9997970

**Mary Newland/Mary Charles:**

The Ships List, The Caucasian (2012).
   http://www.theshipslist.com/ships/australia/caucasian1852.htm
Sidney's Emigrant Journal:
   http://www.ltscotland.org.uk/scotsandaustralia/orphangirls/index.asp

**Joseph Charles:**

The Ships List, The Indian. (2012).
   http://www.theshipslist.com/ships/australia/indian1849.htm
State Library of South Australia. The Indian Affair.
   http://www.slsa.sa.gov.au/fh/passengerlists/1849IndianAffair.htm
Merriam-Webster Dictionary, Chancery: https://www.merriam-webster.com/dictionary/chancery
Description of Westminster:
   http://www.stmw.org/pages/article.asp?Sec=3&S=677&SS=1093&PId=1093

Victorian London - Publications - Social Investigation/Journalism - The Morning Chronicle : Labour and the Poor, 1849-50; Henry Mayhew - Letter XLIII:
   http://www.victorianlondon.org/mayhew/mayhew43.htm
   http://www.victorianlondon.org/mayhew/mayhew45.htm
Old Pye Ragged School: http://www.missing-ancestors.com/

**Deeming Case:**

http://www.prov.vic.gov.au/online-exhibitions/deeming/documents/vprs264-p0-u21-lyleletter2a.htm
http://www.prov.vic.gov.au/online-exhibitions/deeming/documents/vprs264-p0-u21-LyleLetter3.htm

**Daniel Foran:**

B & M Chapman (2003). Soldiers on Garrison Duty (Daniel Foran):
   http://freepages.history.rootsweb.ancestry.com/~garter1/f40th.htm
B & M Chapman (2003). Punishment issued to soldiers:
   http://freepages.history.rootsweb.ancestry.com/~garter1/punishment.htm
Royal Engineers. Life in the British Army. Punishment:
   http://www.royalengineers.ca/Punish.html


**David Gaunson:**

Obituaries Australia, David Gaunson (1846-1909) (from the *West Australian*). http://oa.anu.edu.au/obituary/gaunson-david-3599
David Gaunson, Wikipedia, http://en.wikipedia.org/wiki/David_Gaunson


**Mary MacKillop:**

ABC. (2010). MacKillop banished after uncovering sex abuse.
   http://www.abc.net.au/news/2010-09-25/mackillop-banished-after-uncovering-sex-abuse/2273940
Kensington and Norwood Historical Society, newsletter. Information on Mary MacKillop and Catherine Helen Spence (both lived on Queen Street, Norwood).


**Martha Needle/Martha Charles:**

Macabre Melbourne blog, Cailtin O'Brien. (2010). The tragic tale of Martha Needle (website now defunct).
Bayside city council (2010). History trail, stories in the stones (page now defunct).


**Mental Health and the effects of child sexual abuse:**

Australian Institute of Family Studies. (2013). The long-term effects of child sexual abuse CFCA Paper No. 11 – January 2013. https://aifs.gov.au/cfca/publications/long-term-effects-child-sexual-abuse
Health Line. Fetal alcohol syndrome. What is fetal alcohol syndrome? https://www.healthline.com/health/fetal-alcohol-syndrome


**Post-mortem:**

Post-mortem. (website now defunct). http://www.enotes.com/adipocere-reference/adipocere

**Rigg's Disease and Oral Health:**

Memidex, Rigg's disease: http://www.memidex.com/riggs-diseases


**South Australiana:**

Anlaby homestead. https://anlaby.com.au/

Australian Children's Television Foundation/Education Service Australia. Australia in the 1890s. http://www.myplace.edu.au/decades_timeline/1890/decade_landing_11.html?tabRank=2&subTabRank=1

Boys reformatory. Find and Connect, Boys Reformatory Magill, https://www.findandconnect.gov.au/guide/sa/SE01217

Burra and information on the Lee family. http://www.burrasa.info/

Flinders Ranges Research, Koonunga District. https://www.southaustralianhistory.com.au/koonunga.htm

Flinders Ranges Research, Allen's Creek Bethlehem Lutheran Cemetery. https://www.southaustralianhistory.com.au/allenscreek.htm

The Fitzjames: SA's floating prison for wayward teens, The Advertiser, 3rd May 2017. http://www.adelaidenow.com.au/news/special-features/in-depth/the-fitzjames-sas-floating-prison-for-wayward-teens/news-story/0ec11349685e6ed09ec1152f0192300

State Library of South Australia, The Manning Index of South Australian History. Allen Creek. http://www.slsa.sa.gov.au/manning/pn/a/a6.htm#allenc

State Library of South Australia. The Manning Index of South Australian History. South Australia – Transport. http://www.slsa.sa.gov.au/manning/sa/trans/coaches.htm

State Library of South Australia. The Manning Index of South Australian History. The place names of South Australia. http://www.slsa.sa.gov.au/manning/pn/a/a.htm

Pastoral Pioneers of South Australia. https://www.findmypast.com.au/articles/world-records/full-list-of-australia-and-new-zealand-records/newspapers-directories-and-social-history/south-australia-pastoral-pioneers-of-sa

Postcards SA. Lake Hamilton Eating House: Eyre Peninsula region on the West Coast of South Australia. http://www.postcards-sa.com.au/features/lake_hamilton.html

West Torrens Council. Gateway City, Chapter 3 on 1890s Depression 'The Struggle Years' (pages 30-39) from West Torrens council website. www.wtcc.sa.gov.au/site

Willows Winery. http://www.postcards.sa.com.au/features/willows_winery.html

**Waxworks:**

Waxworks (page now defunct). http://www.glenrowan1880.com/ wax.htm

<u>Newspapers and gazettes:</u>

(Australian Newspapers primarily via National Library of Australia, Newspapers Trove. https://trove.nla.gov.au/newspaper/ and New Zealand Newspapers via National Library of New Zealand, Papers Past. https://paperspast.natlib.govt.nz/)

**The Adelaide Chronicle**

1st May, 1920
12th June, 1920
19th June, 1920

**The Adelaide Chronicle and Weekly Times**

July 1876

**The Adelaide Observer**

3rd January, 1874, cited in  www.sapolicehistory.org/July04.html

**The Advertiser (South Australia)**

15th June 1861
6th September, 1861
14th June 1894
16th June 1894
27th May, 1889
27th June 1889, pg. 3
5th June 1890, pg. 3
17th November 1903, pg. 11
5th November 1906, pg. 10
24th June, 1909, pg. 9
6th January 1913, pg. 14
2nd April 1920
3rd April, 1920
16th April, 1920
17th April, 1920, pg. 9
11th June, 1920, pg. 8

12th June, 1920
18th June, 1920, pg. 6
19th June 1920, pg. 2
21st June, 1920, pg. 10
26th June, 1920, pg. 14
29th June, 1920, pg. 6
30th June 1920, pg. 10
6th July 1920, pg. 10
10th July 1920, pg. 17
12th July 1920, pg. 11
3rd November, 1924
15th June, 2008


**The Age, Melbourne**

12th October, 1988


**The Argus, Melbourne**

6th November 1856, pg. 5
14th June 1894, pg. 5
15th June 1894, pg. 5
16th June 1894, pg. 5, 7
18th June 1894, pg. 5
19th June 1894, pg. 5
20th June 1894, pg. 5
21st June 1894, pg. 4, 5
22nd June 1894, pg. 5
23rd June 1894, pg. 7
25th June 1894, pg. 5
26th June 1894, pg. 6
27th June 1894, pg. 5
30th June 1894, pg. 7
2nd July 1894, pg. 5
3rd July 1894, pg. 6
5th July 1894, pg. 5
6th July 1894, pg. 5
10th July 1894, pg. 5
11th July 1894
12th July 1894, pg. 5
13th July 1894, pg. 5
14th July 1894, pg. 7
17th July 1894, pg. 6

20<sup>th</sup> July 1894, pg. 4, 5
21<sup>st</sup> July 1894, pg. 7
23<sup>rd</sup> July 1894, pg. 5
25<sup>th</sup> July 1894, pg. 5
1<sup>st</sup> August 1894
2<sup>nd</sup> August 1894, pg. 6
3<sup>rd</sup> August 1894, pg. 7
25<sup>th</sup> September 1894, pg. 7
26<sup>th</sup> September, 1894, pg. 7
27<sup>th</sup> September, 1894, pg. 7
28<sup>th</sup> September 1894, pg. 6
29<sup>th</sup> September, 1894, pg. 6
2<sup>nd</sup> October, 1894, pg. 3
10<sup>th</sup> October 1894, pg. 5
15<sup>th</sup> October 1894, pg. 5
17<sup>th</sup> October 1894, pg. 4, 5
22<sup>nd</sup> October, 1894, pg. 5
24<sup>th</sup> October 1894, pg. 5
27<sup>th</sup> October, 1894
30<sup>th</sup> October, 1894
22<sup>nd</sup> November, 1894, pg. 5
6<sup>th</sup> June, 1903, pg. 9
4<sup>th</sup> September 1903, pg. 9
27<sup>th</sup> October 1906, pg. 8
9<sup>th</sup> November 1903, pg. 3
3<sup>rd</sup> April 1920, pg. 12
5<sup>th</sup> April 1920, pg. 6
9<sup>th</sup> June 1920, pg. 9
13<sup>th</sup> April 1920, pg. 7
17<sup>th</sup> April 1920, pg. 21
11<sup>th</sup> June 1920, pg. 7
12<sup>th</sup> June 1920, pg. 20
15<sup>th</sup> June 1920, pg. 4
17<sup>th</sup> June 1920, pg. 8
16<sup>th</sup> July 1920, pg. 8

## The Australasian

23<sup>rd</sup> June, 1894
21<sup>st</sup> July, 1894
23<sup>rd</sup> July, 1894
31<sup>st</sup> August 1895

**The Barrier Miner**
1$^{st}$ August 1894

**Bay of Plenty Times, NZ**
Vol XX11, Issue 3201, 30$^{th}$ November 1894

**The Camperdown Chronicle**
9$^{th}$ October 1894

**The Courier, Qld**
4$^{th}$ October, 1861
6$^{th}$ July 1894, pg. 5

**The Evening Standard**
14$^{th}$ July 1894

**The Geelong Advertiser**
2$^{nd}$ August 1894
27$^{th}$ September, 1894

**The Horsham Times**
10$^{th}$ August 1894

**The Mail**
17$^{th}$ July 1920, pg. 2

**The Mercury**
15$^{th}$ June 1894, pg. 2
30$^{th}$ June 1894, pg. 3
18$^{th}$ June 1920, pg. 8
16$^{th}$ July 1920, pg. 6

**The New York Times**
16$^{th}$ June 1894

**The Pictorial Australian**

May June 1894

**Port Adelaide News and Le Fevre Peninsula Advertiser**

November 1894

**The Register (SA)**

29th November 1839
1st September, 1849, pg. 3
11th March, 1876
15th June 1894
18th June 1894
20th June 1894
22nd March 1920
15th June 1920
18th June, 1920, pg. 7

**SA Police Gazette, Adelaide**

4th December, 1863
15th April, 1864
15th March, 1876
12th April 1876
22nd August 1877
8th September 1880
27th October, 1880
15th December, 1880
8th March, 1882
14th August, 1895

**SA Government Gazette**

31st May, 1860
23rd August 1860.
South Australian Gazetteer, 1866, at
    http://morgan.org.au/html/history.html

**Sandringham/Brighton Advertiser**

16th September, 1996

**The Sydney Morning Herald**

23$^{rd}$ September, 1861
16$^{th}$ June 1894, pg. 10
14$^{th}$ July 1894
25$^{th}$ September, 1894, pg. 5

**Sunday Herald**

13$^{th}$ Nov 1994

**Truth and Progress**

1$^{st}$ November, 1894

**Wanganui Herald, NZ**

Vol XXV111, Issue 8615, 26$^{th}$ October 1894, 18$^{th}$ November, 1894

**The Weekly Times**

23$^{rd}$ June 1894
29$^{th}$ September 1894
13$^{th}$ October, 1894
27$^{th}$ October 1894

CPSIA information can be obtained
at www.ICGtesting.com
Printed in the USA
LVHW091518140619
621259LV00003B/456/P